Rethinking Contemporary British Women's Writing

Rethinking Contemporary British Women's Writing

Realism, Feminism, Materialism

Emilie Walezak

BLOOMSBURY ACADEMIC
LONDON • NEW YORK • OXFORD • NEW DELHI • SYDNEY

BLOOMSBURY ACADEMIC
Bloomsbury Publishing Plc
50 Bedford Square, London, WC1B 3DP, UK
1385 Broadway, New York, NY 10018, USA
29 Earlsfort Terrace, Dublin 2, Ireland

BLOOMSBURY, BLOOMSBURY ACADEMIC and the Diana logo are trademarks of Bloomsbury Publishing Plc

First published in Great Britain 2022
This paperback edition published 2023

Copyright © Emilie Walezak, 2022

Emilie Walezak has asserted her right under the Copyright, Designs and Patents Act, 1988, to be identified as Author of this work.

For legal purposes the Acknowledgements on p. vi constitute an extension of this copyright page.

Cover design by Eleanor Rose
Cover image: *The Black Marble Clock*, c.1870 (oil on canvas) by Cezanne, Paul (1839–1906) © Bridgeman Images

All rights reserved. No part of this publication may be reproduced or transmitted in any form or by any means, electronic or mechanical, including photocopying, recording, or any information storage or retrieval system, without prior permission in writing from the publishers.

Bloomsbury Publishing Plc does not have any control over, or responsibility for, any third-party websites referred to or in this book. All internet addresses given in this book were correct at the time of going to press. The author and publisher regret any inconvenience caused if addresses have changed or sites have ceased to exist, but can accept no responsibility for any such changes.

A catalogue record for this book is available from the British Library.

A catalog record for this book is available from the Library of Congress.

ISBN: HB: 978-1-3501-7135-0
PB: 978-1-3502-5854-9
ePDF: 978-1-3501-7136-7
eBook: 978-1-3501-7137-4

Typeset by Deanta Global Publishing Services, Chennai, India

To find out more about our authors and books visit www.bloomsbury.com and sign up for our newsletters.

Contents

Acknowledgements		vi
1	Introduction: Reading realism anew	1
2	Novel-thinking: Reimagining omniscience	21
3	Abjection, self-abjection and social mutations: Engaging with the reader	43
4	Realist characterization and the feminist politics of location: Situated knowledges	67
5	Realist descriptions: Re-inscribing democracy	91
6	Posthuman naturalism	113
7	The new realist imaginary	137
References		157
Index		172

Acknowledgements

I am deeply grateful to Catherine Bernard for her relentless support and careful advice on the preliminary work initially carried out for the French accreditation to supervise research. It was both an honour and a pleasure to be able to work so closely with Catherine. Thank you to Jean-Michel Ganteau, Vanessa Guignery, Catherine Lanone, Laurent Mellet and Sara Thornton.

I would like to thank Ben Doyle for supporting this project.

My thanks to Guillaume (x Mucha), as always. Thank you to my mother who first gave me *Small Island* at a time when English books were hard to come by in France.

1

Introduction
Reading realism anew

The world today is facing an escalation of emergencies that tie in together the climate, social justice and political models: every year, the Global Footprint Network measures the alarming rate at which planetary resources are being consumed, furthering the gap between the high-income North and the low-income South; the 2019 UN report on the unprecedented decline of the planet's biodiversity was meant to promote a different set of values equating the preservation of ecosystems with social equity against the neoliberal deregulations of the market place. Meanwhile, democratic systems all over the world are at risk. More recently, the 2020 Covid pandemic has put a stop to the global economy and the populations' right to move and travel.

How does literature address those issues? The novel has been theorized historically as appearing simultaneously with democracy, and philosophically as the literary expression of a political system where everyone was to be represented. The realist novel was particularly attuned to depicting the ordinary lives of common people. And it was attacked precisely for those reasons when suspicious critiques started to cast doubt on the replication of a system that submitted people to mindless daily routines.

Today, however, the daily texture of life as we knew it is being impacted by global upheavals: it has become a risk area where everyone can experience for themselves the detrimental effects of climate change through floods, heat waves and so forth. It is also turning into the potential location from which to initiate emancipatory changes for the future by assuming one's personal liability within a more global accountability. What mirror does the contemporary realist novel hold up to the reader? Is it really the reassuring image of a normative society as social constructionists would have it? Doesn't the novel today own up to the challenges we collectively face?

This book aims to demonstrate the vitality and the relevance of the realist genre in experimenting with the connections between individual and collective voices, human and non-human mediations, local and global scales, author and reader. Moreover it contends that women writers are taking an even firmer stand in their aesthetic choice to depict reality considering the detrimental reception where realist novels by women are concerned. It is my contention that the critical paths of new feminist materialism and posthumanism that have emerged these past decades in response to a dissatisfaction with the material/discursive dichotomy upheld by social construction theories have been reflected in the literary practices of women writers for quite some time. This book will take examples from the works of renowned realist women writers such as Pat Barker, A. S. Byatt, Andrea Levy and Rose Tremain to illustrate this point. Furthermore, those new ways of envisaging our place in the world are currently gaining ground in the work of post-millennial writers attuned to the ever more pressing issues of the globalized world, climate change and global interconnectivity. The book will thus also examine the works of such millennial writers as Bernardine Evaristo, Sarah Hall and Zadie Smith. The concluding chapter will furthermore reference the works of emerging writers like Sarah Moss and Melissa Harrison.

The study of literary realism has been lastingly impacted by the poststructuralist critique. The habitual critical stance concerning realism can be summed up thus: the conventional aesthetics of the realist text are deemed to be a mirror of its political conservatism. Criticism is even harsher where women writers are concerned as, in the wake of French feminism, linguistic subversion came to be the standard of feminine writing so that realist women novelists were seen as colluding with the liberal system of patriarchy. The postmodernist moment befittingly referred to that earlier modernist revolution of language that was also conceived of as a political engagement. To put it briefly, while modernism exalted the life of the mind against the middlebrow consumption of mass culture, postmodernism sought to expose the constructedness of all cultural artefacts to shake off the yoke of ideology. Heralding the death of the novel effectively meant doing away with the realist novel. And yet realist novels continued to flourish. Critique, however, has remained indebted to the 1970s epistemological revolutions so that, despite the attempts at rehabilitation mounted by such famed scholars as Raymond Tallis or Andrzej Gasiorek, the reception of realist novels, and especially those written by women novelists, still labours under the discomfort inherited from the social constructionist parallel between aesthetic conformity and reactionary orthodoxy.

Thus Pat Barker, A. S. Byatt and Andrea Levy only came to the attention of the academia when they turned to historiographic metafiction, colouring what is standardly considered as naïve realism with a sophisticated self-reflexivity about knowledge power structures. Still the reception of these writers evidences the difficulty of acknowledging realism as a driving force of their writing. The realist dimension of Byatt's *Possession* was thus attacked on the grounds of its normative impulse, especially in relation to sexuality. Such scholars as Jackie Buxton, Helen Davies or Lisa Fletcher, to quote but a few, all insist on the reactionary 'politics of heteronormativity' sponsored by the 'related narrative structure' (Fletcher 2016: 149). Fletcher, who quotes Catherine Belsey's article 'Reading Love Stories', thus associates the reader's satisfaction with the realist narrative structure as 'the pleasure of reading itself, [is] the pleasure [. . .] of reading classic realist fiction' (Belsey 1992: 141).

About Pat Barker's predominantly realist narratives, Pam Morris has asked:

> current critical thinking has difficulty in fully accommodating and appreciating the writing of a novelist like Pat Barker, whose powerful novels such as *Union Street* (1992) or *The Regeneration Trilogy* (1991–5) are written predominantly in the realist mode. Despite its radical themes and import, must we write off Barker's work as cognitively and aesthetically conservative and hence complicit with existing structures of authority and power? (Morris 2003: 43)

Rose Tremain has not garnered much academic attention because, as Sue Sorensen underlined, 'ambitious and risk-taking in her characters and events, she is less experimental in language and structure than many of her contemporaries' (Sorensen 2015). The enduring bones of contention whenever the issue of realism arises are thus outlined: its purported aversion to experimentation and hence its complicity with dominant norms, its middlebrow focus supposedly addressing a naïve reader, its characteristic conventions allegedly confining it to a submissive adherence to the powers that be. And yet realist novels continue to prosper. As Nick Turner wrote, 'realism is a protean form that should not be dismissed, for our leading novelists are writing within the realist mode, and implicitly questioning its unfashionable status' (Turner 2013: 51). It is this book's contention that not only are writers reinventing realism today but that there are also new ways of reading realism. Furthermore, while the new readings this book will offer would apply to male and female writers alike, its focus is on women novelists because, as Chapter 2 will demonstrate, they take the brunt of harsh criticism. To put it simply, because their reception can be particularly affected by the inherited misconceptions about realism, it is then a reader's task to read anew, or as Nick Turner stated in his book on *Post-War British Novelists and the Canon*: 'it is not new to say that women writers are and have been undervalued in literature; however, it does still need to be said' (Turner 2010: 2). However while the book will address gender and race issues, this is not its main purpose.

Its main purpose will be to pursue innovative reading ventures with the help of the new material feminist and posthuman theories that aim to outline the material agency of human and non-human bodies to challenge the body/mind split inherited from Cartesian dualism. Because those theories primarily refer to the legacy of the linguistic turn, the book will reference the critiques of realism that arose in the wake of Saussure's theory of the arbitrariness of the sign and were inspired by the works of Roland Barthes, Jacques Lacan and Louis Althusser.

Why then do women writers persist in depicting the world realistically against the critical concept of its discursive constructedness? Maybe because matter matters, to quote Karen Barad's catchphrase that has become the motto of new materialism; or, as A. S. Byatt put it, to capture the 'thingness' of things (Byatt 1993: 9). Women writing realistically testify to an attempt to reconcile the challenges of embodied experience with the disputes of social constructions. This book uses the widespread consensus on the codes that typify realism and aims to read anew the use of those conventions in contemporary women's writing with the help of those theories that developed after the paradigmatic changes effected by feminist, postcolonial and environmental epistemologies: 'Feminist, postcolonial, and environmental epistemologies have long critiqued modes of knowing that install a gap between the subject and the object of knowledge' (Alaimo 2014: 15). Thus the definition of realism used in this book is based on its narrative devices and stylistic procedures explored in the following chapters: omniscience, third-person and first-person narratives, temporal and spatial causality, the psychological verisimilitude of characterization, and the real-life accuracy of descriptions. The realist novel today reinvents modes of knowing and of describing reality by representing the empirical experiences of embodied subjects.

When challenging the gap between body and mind, posthuman theorists frequently turn to Spinoza's monism as promoting an agential view of matter as living matter not bound in oppositions but as a crucible of interacting differences. It is a lay interpretation of Spinoza that uses science and technology to overcome the body/mind divide: 'For instance, a neo-Spinozist approach is supported and expanded today by new developments in the mind-body interrelation within the neural sciences (Damasio, 2003)' (Braidotti 2013: 57). A. S. Byatt has written a review of Antonio Damasio's book, *Looking for Spinoza*, in which she develops the concept of the 'embodied mind' that informs her latest writing (Byatt 2003a) reshaping the body/mind dilemma that characterized her early novels. She further calls on neurosciences as an analogy for her writing work which uses scientific lexicons as varied as that of entomology, geology or oceanography, to design new taxonomies that delineate knowing embodied subjects. The notion of embodiment is crucial to a fresh understanding of realism today and writers like Zadie Smith experiment with the voices of realism to reconcile knowing and feeling. Smith has referenced George Eliot's attempted translation of Spinoza's *Ethics* as the thinking process behind *Middlemarch*. Realist fiction allows to couch cogitations in embodied subjectivities accessed through omniscience.

In scientific studies, this gap is echoed in the divide between the object of study and the knowing subject. It is no coincidence that some of the major figures of new material feminism are feminist scientists themselves. Donna Haraway used her background as a biologist to contest the disembodied scientific intelligence. In her ground-breaking article from 1988, 'Situated Knowledges: The Science Question in Feminism and the Privilege of Partial Perspective', she developed the concept of 'material–semiotic nodes' to approach bodies and feminist embodiment in particular. She parallels the feminist history of women's objectification with the modern scientific stance of detached observation to collapse the distinction between subject and object. It is a feminist gesture of challenging conceptions of subjectivity by appropriating one's objectified status. Instead of considering subject and object as distinct, Haraway offers a view of the bodies as happening at the nodal point where language and matter meet: 'Like "poems," which are sites of literary production where language too is an actor independent of intentions and authors, bodies as objects of knowledge are material–semiotic generative nodes. Their *boundaries* materialize in social interaction. Boundaries are drawn by mapping practices; "objects" do not pre-exist as such. Objects are boundary projects' (Haraway 1988: 595). By describing and questioning current social mutations, realism, too, engages in 'mapping practices'. True to its original focus on common people and everyday routines, the realist novel has been transformed by the epistemological revolutions of feminism, postcolonialism and environmentalism. Women writers use the realist tools of empathetic and antipathetic characterization to tackle the gender and race divides. Their narratives of various characters' trajectory registers their struggle with social transformations. Rose Tremain, Pat Barker and Andrea Levy are keen to portray antipathetic characters that cannot cope with the world's changes alongside emancipatory stories of successful conversions. Sarah Hall uses the geographic boundaries of her native region of Cumbria to map the interrelations between its human and non-human populations – landscapes included – and dramatizes their embodied struggles with the disincarnate decision-making bodies of state and regional administration. Her writing strives to outline the reciprocal imprints of embodiment and embeddedness.

The physicist Karen Barad has developed the concept of 'agential intra-actions' between 'material-discursive forces' which is very similar to Haraway's nodes (Barad 2003: 810). Barad uses the term 'intra-action' to defeat the notion that entities pre-exist, which the term 'interaction' presupposes. Instead she envisages the phenomena that emerge in the encounter between matter and language. Her conception is based on Niels Borh's quantum physics notion that objects and agencies of observation are inseparable in quantum measurements and that describes the processes rather than the states of the particles (Barad 2010). Barad is thus also a posthumanist in that she means to accord agency to human and non-human forces alike. Her goal is to upset the familiar coordinates of thought, including time, space and causality. Barad's 'agential realism' bears strong resemblances to Jane Bennett's 'vibrant materialism' which similarly considers the agency of matter itself (Bennett 2010). Bennett references Spinoza's monism. She also calls on the new materialism of Bruno Latour and his actor-network theory when she writes about matter as an 'actant'. The aim of both Barad and Bennett is to design new onto-epistemologies. Contemporary short fiction is particularly suited to the purpose of delivering 'onto-stories' (Bennett 2010), narrating the entanglements of organic and inorganic matter like Byatt's 'A Stone Woman' or her latest 'Sea Story' (2013), or the enmeshment of the human and the animal as in the stories of Sarah Hall, 'Bees' and 'Mrs Fox'. While the question of ontology might necessitate a deviation from the realist frame to allow for uncommon transmutations, it is my contention that the writers' short stories intra-act with their novels so that their short fiction sheds light on poetic skills honed and condensed, in particular their work with analogy that defeats taxonomic hierarchies.

In the humanities, the body/mind divide is mirrored in the hiatus between words and things. The collection Stacy Alaimo and Susan Hekman edited in 2008, *Material Feminisms*, was meant to address the blind spot of postmodern feminism: 'Although postmoderns claim to reject all dichotomies, there is one dichotomy that they appear to embrace almost without question: language/reality' (Alaimo and Hekman 2008: 2). Because bodies and nature in their material dimension have long served essentialist scientific discourses, postmodern feminisms have focused on the discursive construction of constraining social models. New material feminism rehabilitates thinkers like Luce Irigaray to investigate our bodily natures as creative loci of interacting differences whose complex materiality further resonates with the world's bodies. Stacy Alaimo drew on Haraway's and Barad's concepts to develop her theory of transcorporeality in order to 'think as a body' as 'the posthuman being is entangled with the very stuff of the word' (Alaimo 2014: 16). Transcorporeality is meant to emphasize at one and the same time human embodiment and environmental embeddedness: 'Imagining human corporeality as trans-corporeality, in which the human is always intermeshed with the more-than-human world, underlines the extent to which the substance of the human is ultimately inseparable from "the environment"' (Alaimo 2010: 2). This permeability is echoed in the notion of 'viscous porosity' developed by Nancy Tuana in Alaimo and Hekman's collection:

> There is a viscous porosity of flesh – my flesh and the flesh of the world. This porosity is a hinge through which we are of and in the world. I refer to it as viscous, for there are membranes that effect these interactions. These membranes are of various types – skin and flesh, prejudgements and symbolic imaginaries, habits and embodiments. They serve as the mediators of interactions. (Tuana 2008: 199–200)

The careful attention given to the 'mesh' (Morton 2010) of interconnectedness between all things, human and non-human, living and dead, is mirrored in the meticulous work of realist descriptions. Pat Barker's work with viscous fluids means to rupture the borders between the intimate and the public to transcribe the experience of rape thus expressing the resonance between the individual consciousness and the 'stuff of the world' (Alaimo 2014). Zadie Smith and Bernardine Evaristo relish in the description of fabrics, the literal textures of fashion items, to bring to the fore the visibility issue where

Black women are concerned, thus weaving together the material, the social and the textual (Latour 1993: 7). Byatt's characteristic ekphrases outline the reciprocal contact between the self and the world, thus offering a way out of ego-bound solipsism, turning instead to an aesthetic and sensory appreciation of the details of the material world. The work with metonymy, that Roman Jakobson singled out as typifying realist writing, abolishes hierarchical distinctions by emphasizing the contiguity of relationships and serves to implement an 'ambient poetics' (Morton 2007) by 'metonymically digress[ing] from the plot to the atmosphere and from the characters to the setting in space and time' (Jakobson 2003: 43).

Considering being affected – or infected – finally has a potential for new democratic redistributions. It is also the object of Jane Bennett's vibrant materialism. Bennett uses Jacques Rancière's theory of the partition of the sensible and enlarges it to 'the thing-power' of the non-humans:

> Theories of democracy that assume a world of active substances and passive objects begin to appear as thin descriptions at a time when the interactions between human, viral, animal, and technological bodies are becoming more and more intense. If human culture is inextricably enmeshed with vibrant, nonhuman agencies, and if human intentionality can be agentic only if accompanied by a vast entourage of nonhumans, then it seems that the appropriate unit of analysis for democratic theory is neither the individual human nor an exclusively human collective but the (ontologically heterogeneous) 'public' coalescing around a problem. (Bennett 2010: 108)

A change of paradigm is occurring today, largely prompted by an increased awareness of depleted biodiversity and unprecedented atmospheric changes, which challenges our perception and understanding of reality. Even though Haraway rightly singles out science fiction as an apt vehicle to translate the technocultures we live in, it is my contention that the current need for new descriptions of the tangled stuff of the world can also find an appropriate intermediary in the realist novel.

Instead of the critical view that considers the conventional aesthetics of the realist text to be a mirror of its political conservatism, the book aims to promote the notion that the realist text today is a means of choice for writers registering the ongoing process of re-description, and henceforth redefinition, of nature, whether human or non-human, male, female or other. In addition, the fictional embodied experiences narrated by the women writers under study address the practical issues of gender, race and kind. That they opt for realist narrative and stylistic devices demonstrates the current need to rethink our views on reality, both epistemologically speaking as thinking bodies and ontologically speaking as interconnected agencies. Thus the first four chapters are conceived as a dialogue between the former critique of realism and novel readings calling on new material feminism and posthumanism while the last two chapters address more specifically the ecological issue.

Chapter 2 pits the long-established view of omniscience as authoritarian, which led to the postmodern experiments with self-reflexive authors/writers playfully exposing their own controlling presence, against an ethical reconsideration of the writers' role in the extra-diegetic democratic debate. This established view was largely expounded by Catherine Belsey who developed Roland Barthes's argument that readerly novels – of which the realist novel is the paradigmatic example – comfort the reader with the verisimilitude of a bourgeois perspective on the world: the literary norms of past tense and third-person omniscience manifest the social norms that command the reader's world. Belsey, in turn, suggested that third-person omniscience imposes an authoritarian control over the text forcing the reader to concur with its intended moral and implementing a hierarchy of discourses, with that of the author–narrator purported to be the valid one. The third-person narrator of Zadie Smith's *White Teeth* fuelled numerous debates and inspired James Wood's famous critique of hysterical realism. Wood deplored a 'crisis of character' in the contemporary novel which he attributed, in Smith's case, to the intrusive voice of a satirical narrator that 'obliterates' its characters.

The chapter aims to demonstrate instead how writers like A. S. Byatt and Zadie Smith have been engaging critically with the issue of realism in their non-fiction and how their extra-textual voices parallel their fictional use of omniscience, not as an instrument of control, but as an empathetic means to access the consciousnesses of vast casts of characters. In her non-fictional writing, Smith obsessively deliberates the dualistic dissociation of the readerly and the writerly and references George Eliot as her paragon to finding the way to connect feeling and knowing. A. S. Byatt has spent her career looking for a way to escape the solipsism of modernist subjectivity and postmodernist self-reflexivity (Byatt 2000b) and calls on both George Eliot and Iris Murdoch to defend a view of the realist novel as harbouring 'incarnate consciousnesses' (Byatt 2019). By sharing their thought processes with the readers, Byatt and Smith help redefine omniscience not as anthropocentric omnipotence but as community building whereby the 'reality effect' denigrated by Barthes as fallacious, covering up the cultural constructedness of reality, turns into what French philosopher Jacques Rancière has called an 'equality effect' (2014: 26, my translation) that puts on an equal footing common people and everyday objects, writers and readers.

Byatt's irritation with 'the Age of Suspicion' (Byatt 2000b) echoes Rancière's assessment of Althusser's critical heritage, which he calls the critiques of domination, and which, he writes, turned against their initial purpose of overthrowing hierarchical subordination by ultimately opposing the erudite and the unaware (Rancière 2012: 12). Precisely, Raymond Tallis had previously criticized Belsey's Althuserrian reading that the realist text would smother contradiction by imposing the transcendental view of the omniscient narrator (Tallis 1988: 79–88), emphasizing instead the role of the realist novel in raising the awareness of its original readers to social struggles. He points out how Belsey's critique of the hierarchy of discourses is replaced by a new hierarchy between readers: the expert reader versus the naïve reader (Tallis 1988: 152–3). Rita Felski has also cast doubt on what she calls the hermeneutics of suspicion which colour negatively anything deemed to be conventional or familiar:

> It is one thing to point out that certain ideas are bad and also taken for granted. It is another to conclude that they are bad because they are taken for granted – in other words that anything taken for granted is an agent of domination. Such an antinature animus, with its unblinking suspicion of anything tainted by convention, has the effect of assigning an automatically backward status to everyday language. (Felski 2015: 80)

The chapter engages with the new materialist contestation of 'the critiques of domination', that focused on demystification, to advocate for a new reading of realist conventions that wonders at the possibilities offered by omniscience to connect empathetically. The chapter uses Jacques Rancière's notion of the distribution of the sensible as the bedrock of new materialist theories to record an ongoing epistemological change in our perception of reality that seeks to go beyond the body/mind divide.

Chapter 3 explores further the relationship with the reader, arguing that contemporary realism seeks to implement a new reader compact based on affect. It proposes to reinterpret Julia Kristeva's abjection theory to shed light on the contemporary re-appropriation of literary naturalism.

In the 1980s, Kristeva's use of Bakhtin and her conceptualization of the abject (see Vice 1997), aimed to bare social taboos and prohibitions in relation to bodily representations, gave rise to the female grotesque theory (Russo 1995). While classic realism, with its alleged unproblematic relationship to referentiality, was interpreted as the perpetuation of a phallocentric value system – as Catherine Belsey's comparison of the characterization of Dorothea in *Middlemarch* to a perfume ad strategy demonstrates (Belsey 2002: 46–7) – feminist scholars turned to magic realism as the genre par excellence with which to upset the 'natural' values traditionally associated with femininity and to thus capsize essentialism. As a consequence, attention focused on the fantastic, Gothic or otherwise supernatural elements that came to trouble the comfort of readerly texts. This is the case with Pat Barker's reception in particular. John Brannigan, for instance, interprets the supernatural in Pat Barker's novels as the disturbing element that shatters the gratification of contented realist reading: 'In all of her novels, there are scenes which could easily be described as social realism, representing quotidian experiences in almost documentary detail, but they are always interspersed or perforated with tropes of the extraordinary, supernatural or spectral, which trouble the comfortable readerly experience of verisimilitudinous realism' (Brannigan 2005a: 173).

This chapter contends that Pat Barker, Andrea Levy and Rose Tremain use abjection not to contest social models of conformity as in postmodern feminist writing but to shock the readers, through antipathetic feelings, into realizing the internalized self-detestation of the minorities, especially women and Black people. Barker and Tremain reinterpret the naturalist investigation of human baseness with a feminist view that seeks to expose a collective complicity in degrading women. They reconnect with the initial scandalous nature of realism and naturalism. Both writers reference the classic nineteenth century founding figures of Émile Zola, Honoré de Balzac or Charles Dickens. Neo-characterization in Tremain's texts, by importing past character types in the novel's present (Letissier 2015), challenges the readers' expectations as well as their social views. Barker gestures towards Angela Carter's moral pornography by forcing her reader to experience a rapist's point of view in *Blow Your House Down*. Focalization is instrumental in engaging the readers' affects and it is up to them to decide whether to accord the characters the redemption some of them are looking for. Responsibility for the other is thus relocated in the readers themselves. Pornography, abuse and impropriety are used to raise the readers' awareness of their own liability in fighting or collaborating with social inequity.

In *Small Island*, Andrea Levy uses affective focalization to expose racism by exhibiting its abjectifying process. She engineers complex reader identifications that walk the thin line between attraction and repulsion to engage the readers into confronting their own prejudices. The chapter aims to rehabilitate the common reader that the realist novel was first intended for, against the prejudiced suspicion against them inherited from the modernist critique of mass culture as outlined in Virginia Woolf's scathing essay on the middlebrow (Woolf 1942). Thus, in her analysis of average reader responses to Levy's novel gathered from book clubs, Anouk Lang connects the lack of formal inventiveness of the realist genre of the novel with its middlebrow prosperity in the form of radio and film adaptations to question the standards of academic consideration:

> Viewing the text through the eyes of its readers [. . .] gestures towards a wider issue in postcolonial studies, of 'what counts' as a text worth reading, teaching and writing about. Being largely realist and without much formal inventiveness *Small Island* is likely to be of less interest to literary critics than denser and more overtly stylized texts. Moreover, it risks being dismissed as middle-brow or mainstream, especially given that it has been validated by several arbiters of middle-brow, among them award-winning bodies, the BBC (who broadcast it over the radio in shortened and serialized form). (Lang 2009: 138)

The chapter uses the new materialist approach of Rita Felski who developed a phenomenology of reading in *Uses of Literature* to explore how realist characterization both mirrors and debunks our society's prejudices through arousing the reader's empathetic and antipathetic affects.

Chapter 4 pursues the exploration of realist characterization and uses Donna Haraway's concept of situated knowledges to develop both a reading of the fictional incarnation of the concept as well as an extra-diegetic consideration of the novelists' own experiments and evolution from one novel to the next. It investigates more particularly the eventual turn to the first-person narrator in the novels of A. S. Byatt and Zadie Smith and how this pivot might be construed as a step in their fictional endeavours to ethically embody the personal without the ego, to acknowledge the partiality of knowledge without giving up on truth claims, to explore the vagaries of what it means to be human. Because they are aware of producing knowledge through fiction, they experiment with the voices of realism – third- and first-person narratives – to give a fictional embodiment to thinking processes: the aim is to connect empirical experience with incarnate knowledge, for instance through mutual characterization in Smith or through the webs of analogies woven by Byatt.

The chapter also examines Sarah Hall's characteristic and uncommon use of the judiciary in her novels as another example of situating knowledge by 'siting (sighting) boundaries' (Haraway 1988: 595). While Smith explores social boundaries and Byatt investigates those of scientific disciplines, Hall surveys physical borders as the sum of complex geographic, historical, geophysical and legal processes. Her approach to the bodies thus fictionalizes them as 'material–semiotic nodes', and she uses contrastive male and female focalizations to reconnoitre sexual difference.

The realist procedures used by these women novelists are experiments in giving shape to feminist objectivity, that is a way of producing knowledge that makes room for partial perspectives but nevertheless seeks a common ground. Realist fiction, with its investigation of human behaviour, is perfectly suited to delve into the thought processes of characters that come to embody moral concepts.

Chapter 5 continues the reflexion on characters as incarnate ideas by enlarging its consideration of the fictional world to the objects that populate the novels. While Barthes dismissed the '"futile" details' (Barthes 1989: 141) of realist descriptions that, in his view, only served to attest the verisimilitude of the novelistic world, thus contributing to the 'reality effect' of the text, this chapter contends that they serve a democratic purpose of describing the 'world-in-common' (Rancière 2010: 93). Re-distributing the world's textures through modes of attention that care for its details means affecting our perspective on reality by giving renewed consideration to empirical phenomena. The chapter uses the work of feminist epistemologist Elizabeth Grosz who reinterprets Julia Kristeva's abjection and Luce Irigaray's fluid mechanics to develop an understanding of female corporeality as 'a mode of seepage' (1994: 203). Pat Barker's descriptive work with fluids similarly connects her characters' physical sensations with a cultural imaginary to paint the reciprocal imprint of self and world. Her poetics evidences a 'viscous porosity' (Tuana 2008: 199) between the individual corporeal experience and the public social environment that manifests the intangible boundaries that structure reality. While Barker uses description as contaminating abjection, Smith and Evaristo's writing expresses a delight in the use of texturizing adjectives whose jubilance turns into a site of resistance to racism that would mute and make invisible the Black experience. The chapter, in particular, investigates the material–semiotic node of hair in the diversity of its styles and textures whose variety challenges the taxonomies of scientific imperial racism. Byatt's work with taxonomies is also examined in relation to her colour optics. Realist descriptions thus capsize the subject/object relationships questioning the epistemological process of naming the world.

Chapter 6 further investigates the ontological consequences in writing this new democracy of things. It uses the posthuman feminist phenomenology developed by Astrida Neimanis who outlines, after Merleau Ponty's embodied phenomenology, the primacy of empirical experience in the production of knowledge. In order to rethink ontological divides, Neimanis has elaborated in particular the concepts of 'hydrocommons' to designate 'the interbeing of water bodies on this planet' (2017: 161). The chapter reads the work of Sarah Hall in the light of Neimanis's concept to emphasize the writer's mesh of human and macroscopic scales. It further investigates Hall's short fiction that figures transmogrifications of humans into animals and the short fiction of A. S. Byatt, more particularly the geological story 'A Stone Woman' and her most recent narrative of the travel journey of a plastic bottle in 'Sea Story' inspired by a discarded metaphor from her latest novel *Ragnarok*.

The chapter parallels the novel work and the short fiction of A. S. Byatt and Sarah Hall to tackle the ontological dimension of the changing perception of our nature-cultures. It details the poetic procedures that testify to a posthuman turn in contemporary writing with anthropomorphic analogies designed to counter anthropocentric metaphors through processes of becoming: becoming woman, becoming fox, becoming water, becoming stone. Short fiction allows writers to perform more radical metamorphoses that display the fearless vitalism of *zoe*, the raw force of life theorized by Rosi Braidotti as both threatening and generative contagion. Naturalism gets reinterpreted as posthuman naturalism with science serving a post-anthropocentric imaginary of boundary crossings and trans-species assemblages.

Chapter 7 concludes on the new realist imaginaries that are emerging in response to today's environmental and political crises. It focuses in particular on the development of post-pastoral writing and parallels the novels of Sarah Hall with that of emerging writers Sarah Moss and Melissa Harrison who use the rural spaces of England as an environmental terrain imbued with a cultural imaginary that connects to geopolitical issues made urgent by the Brexit context. Their most recent novels inquire into collective denial and complicity in the wake of the Me Too movement and embody the legal issues of land rights and minority rights in their characters, thus engaging the readers in a speculation about the world-in-common. Such mediations on collective liability are mirrored in the writers' experiments with personal pronouns, in particular the second-person pronouns used by Smith and Hall in their short fiction. Harrison's first-person essay, *Rain. Four Walks in English Weather*, appropriates phenomenologically the iconic English weather in a materialist and environmentalist form that gives shape to the weathering imaginary Astrida Neimanis is calling for. Weathering, again, raises the question of human liability in changing meteorological patterns and how going back to an empirical experience of it may pave the way for new justice approaches to human and non-human weather bodies.

Realism matters in appropriating routine as 'a lived relationship' (Felski 1999: 31) in a world that calls for us to transition towards new embodiments and a new sense of embeddedness.

2

Novel-thinking

Reimagining omniscience

The poststructuralist critique of omniscience was based on the equivalence drawn with the omnipotence of the creator. The classic realist text served as a contrastive exemplar to the self-reflexive experimentations of the postmodernist novel. In British fiction, John Fowles's *The French Lieutenant Woman* was hailed by Malcolm Bradbury as the prototype of the metafictional turn in post-war fiction (1993: 351). Bradbury's retrospective argument in *The Modern British Novel* from 1993 was meant to refigure the 1960s perception of British fiction on the international literary scene as insular and conventional. Novels in the 1950s in England, like William Cooper's *Scenes from a Provincial Life*, indeed reclaimed the realist tradition to oppose the modernist experiments (see Wells 2003: 23–42) and were seen as parochial.

By explicitly unveiling the function of the author as an all-powerful agent in the novel's world in chapter 13, which calls on the tutelary figures of Barthes and Robbe-Grillet, Fowles was able to disband the referential illusion and involve the readers in critical thinking about novel writing. Such a metafictional gesture was premised on the notion that the Victorian novel considered the author as a god-like figure. A. S. Byatt's *Possession* was a response to Fowles's novel and to what Byatt considered to be his 'crude understanding' of the

Victorians as she explained in her famous essay, 'People in Paper Houses': 'Fowles's understanding of Victorian life and literature is crude and derived from the Bloomsbury rejection of it, which makes his technical nostalgia fascinating as a phenomenon' (1993: 155).

Byatt points out the British specificity of the debate originating in the modernist revolution. In the same text, she traces the constancy of the line drawn between tradition and innovation and condemns blindsided bias on all sides: 'These irritable territorial definitions have taken place against the background of a critical discussion of contemporary fiction which has been, in this country, decidedly thin; and against a critical lore – and this is important – characteristically moral and prescriptive' (1993: 155). She turns the argument of prescriptive morality against the poststructuralists that used it to censure the realist norm of omniscient narration as a form of authoritarianism. Byatt's own irritability with what she deems to be an insubstantial critical debate testifies to her determination in defending realism at a time when her choice to engage with this tradition implied exposing herself to fierce criticism. 'People in Paper Houses' thus reads as a manifesto for realism. It was originally published in 1979 in Malcolm Bradbury's collection *The Contemporary British Novel*. As evidenced by the many collections edited by Bradbury to establish the narrative of post-war fiction in England, the extra-diegetic debate couched in non-fictional form constantly attended the writers' own fictional undertakings.

For herself, Byatt claims the legacy of Iris Murdoch whose famous text from 1961 'Against Dryness' also constituted a stepping stone in the British debate. Reporting on the state of the novel in the 1960s, Murdoch saw a divide between 'crystalline novels' focusing on fantasy and myths and 'dry novels' adopting the tone of documentary realism. The text was her plea to persist with the ambitions of the great realist novel conceived as the imaginary representation of moral struggles embodied in individual characters. It inspired

David Lodge's 1969 'The Novelist at the Crossroads' in which he advocated for a 'compromise' between fiction and empiricism in the novel, in other words, a hybrid form between the crystalline and the documentary.

Zadie Smith prolonged the debate in 2008 with a text published in the *New York Review of Books* as 'Two Paths for the Novel', reissued a year later as 'Two Directions for the Novel' in the collection of essays *Changing My Mind*. Even though it appears that Zadie Smith sides with experimental fiction by pitting the novelty of McCarthy's *Remainder* against the conventional 'lyrical realism' of O Neill's *Netherland*, her novelistic practice testifies to an attempt to delineate a 'third way' (Holmes 2013). In the same collection of essays, she explains how her mind is divided between her enthusiasm as a reader for Barthes's notion of the writerly and her connection as a writer to Nabokov's view of the author as limiting 'the possibility of the reader's play' (2011: 43) through exercising control over his text.

In yet another piece, she also calls on the realist legacy of George Eliot. The starting point of her defence of Eliot is the criticism of the modernist view of Henry James on *Middlemarch*. James cannot see the relevance of Eliot's large cast of commonplace characters and of the 'fullness of detail' about them (Smith 2011: 28). Smith structures her defence around three main arguments: the notion of equality, enhanced in the piece's title '*Middlemarch* and Everybody', the reciprocity of the author's life and work, in that the author's life experiences helped with the gestation of the novel, and the Spinozist interrelation between knowing and feeling fictionalized by Eliot.

The notion of equality – 'to Eliot all were equal, and of equal interest, and worthy of an equal number of pages' (Smith 2011: 34) – echoes Jacques Rancière's view of the realist novel and of how the poststructuralists misinterpreted its scope (Rancière 2014). The structuralists and the poststructuralists aimed to disrupt the narrative norms epitomized by the classic realist text by calling into question the verisimilitude of representation. However Rancière contends that their arguments not only missed the point of the democratic revolution engineered by the realist novel but also perpetuated, under a new guise, an Aristotelean order of representation that sought a form of adequation between language and subject matter, and established hierarchies (2014: 29–30). For Rancière, on the contrary, the realist novel was the initial disruptive moment when representation was disputed:

> The leap outside of *mimēsis* is by no means the refusal of figurative representation. Furthermore, its inaugural moment has often been called *realism*, which does not in any way mean the valorization of resemblance but rather the destruction of the structures within which it functioned. Thus novelistic realism is first of all the reversal of the hierarchies of representation (the primacy of the narrative over the descriptive or the hierarchy of subject matter) and the adoption of a fragmented or proximate mode of focalization, which imposes raw presence to the detriment of the rational sequences of the story. (2011: 24)

That the omniscient narrator also promotes access to the many consciousnesses of large casts of characters, that the descriptive details deemed superfluous by James and Barthes are in fact a way to picture the real as a variety of 'textures' (Rancière 2014: 28), mean that to Rancière 'the alleged reality effect is rather to be considered as an equality effect' (2014: 26, my translation). All the beings and things represented are put on an equal footing. Thus Rancière deems the realist novel as inaugurating democracy in literature by materializing equality achieved through depicting commonplace people and everyday objects. Classic realist novels have upset existing sensible orders and painted new 'distributions of the sensible'. This is what Smith calls for at the end of her piece when she exhorts readers to not simply dwell nostalgically in the past of Victorian novels but to look for 'the George Eliot of today' (2011: 40).

Art meets politics at 'the level of the sensible delimitation of what is common to the community, the forms of its visibility and of its organization' (Rancière 2011: 18). Contrary to the poststructuralist *doxa* that postulated that the realist novel only mimicked a bourgeois order of things, it is Rancière's contention that the realist novel was of the avant-garde if one considers the avant-garde to be 'not on the side of the advanced detachments of artistic innovation but on the side of the invention of sensible forms and material structures of a life to come' (2011: 29). Quoting Eliot's essay 'Silly Novels by Lady Novelists', Smith reminds us that 'George Eliot may look cosy and conservative from a century's distance, but she was on the border of the New – so will her descendants be' (2011: 40).

Smith means to refigure experience in the realist novel. It is significant that she insists on Eliot's own experiences that helped gestate *Middlemarch*, in particular Eliot's effort at translating Spinoza's *Ethics*. Smith reads *Middlemarch* as the fictional embodiment of Spinoza's *conatus*. Eliot depicts characters striving to find the right way of being in the world. Their striving mirrors Eliot's own life experiences of which Smith says *Middlemarch* is the sum. Smith's experiment with realist fiction is her own striving, weaving together thought and feeling: '*feeling into knowledge, knowledge into feeling*' (2011: 40). It is a constantly gestating process related to her life experiences: the title of the collection of essays, *Changing My Mind*, testifies to this fluid, dynamic process of thinking through affect in novel writing.

Christopher Holmes has called this process in Smith's work 'novel-thinking' (2013: 142). Basing himself on Smith's responses to James Wood, Holmes reads in Smith's essays 'an implicit argument for form's possibility not as a representational agent, but as structuring model for future forms of thought' (2013: 145). This is similar to the distinction operated by Rancière between the logic of representation on the one hand and the aesthetic regime on the other. In the logic of representation, mimesis is 'not an artistic process but a regime of visibility regarding the arts', 'a fold in the distribution of ways of doing and making as well as in social occupations, a fold that renders the arts visible' (2011: 22). In the aesthetic regime, 'the identification of art no longer occurs via a division within ways of doing and making, but it is based on distinguishing a sensible mode of being specific to artistic products' (2011: 22). Smith's striving to articulate feeling and knowing fluidly in fiction is her way of devising new epistemologies and new ontologies for the present.

The relationship between feeling and knowing is also reminiscent of Fredrick Jameson's recent change of mind concerning realism. In *Postmodernism, or the Cultural Logic of Late Capitalism* Jameson deemed the realist novel to be the product of the first industrial phase of capitalism as opposed to the later modernist and postmodernist forms. In his book from 2015, *The Antinomies of Realism*, he reneges on his own historical periodization to consider realism as an 'anomaly' (2015: 6). Jameson approaches realism as a hybrid form constantly becoming undone and which rests on the tension between 'récit' and affect. Jameson's definition could be likened to the 'novel-thinking' Holmes descries in Smith's work: thinking the realist novel, as Jameson does, as an 'aporia' (2015: 6) means thinking of the novel as an intermediary. Quoting Rita Felski's piece inspired by the new materialist conceptions of Bruno Latour, Holmes suggests that 'Smith's writing endeavours [. . .] to read the novel, as Rita Felski has suggested in 'Context Stinks!', not as something to be known but as something to know with' (2013: 142). This is the reason why Smith insists on the gestating process of Eliot which is exceptionally accessible through the journal Eliot wrote at the time when she was working on *Middlemarch*.

This chapter makes a parallel between two famous realist women novelists, A. S. Byatt and Zadie Smith, on the basis of their shared appetite to engage their readers in partaking in their thinking process through the many non-fictional pieces they write for the press and which end up collected as essays. It argues furthermore that their practice of essay writing is consistent with their realist practice in fiction as the writer's voice used in the essays prolongs that of the omniscient narrator in the novels. Byatt and Smith are both powerful intellectual figures whose moral involvement with the world is reflected in the correlation between their novels and their essays, in short their 'novel-thinking'. Richard Dawson has analysed the reappearance of omniscience in contemporary fiction as 'a performance of narrative authority' which means to connect the fictional world with 'the extradiegetic or public world of the readers' (2009: 146). For Dawson, 'it is possible, then, to establish a discursive continuum from narratorial commentary on a work of fiction to critical pronouncements in a work of nonfiction which establish mutually reinforcing claims for an author's cultural capital' (2009: 151).

While Byatt's essays in *Passions of the Mind* preceded the publication of her acclaimed *Possession*, with 'People in Paper Houses' dating back to 1979, she later wrote about the gestalt of the Booker prize-winning novel to further explain her narrative choices in answer to her readers' responses. The use of the omniscient narrator in the novel's epilogue, which reveals that Ash met his daughter and was aware of her existence, in particular, angered many readers: 'I still receive angry letters from time to time from all over the world, saying these passages are a mistake, [. . .] and that I am breaking my own convention incompetently. But my decision was very deliberate' (Byatt 1995c). Byatt assumes her choice as polemical in a bid to defend access to the characters' affect:

> I also believe the third-person narrator has been much maligned in the recent past – it does not pretend to 'God' – simply the narrative voice which knows what it does know. And I wanted to show that such a voice can bring the reader closer to the passions and the thoughts of characters, without any obligation to admire the cleverness of the novelist. (1995c)

She clearly refers to the opposite metafictional self-consciousness of author-narrators like Fowles's which display the brilliance of the novelist reflecting on his work. Her insistence on her writer's choices is all the more significant as she is regularly accused of being too clever, elitist or condescending. For instance, her latest book from 2016, *Peacock and Vine*, which is halfway between a biographic essay on the lives and works of William Morris and Mariano Fortuny, and an 'auctorbiography' (Chevalier 1999: 19) about the workings of her creative imagination, received harsh criticism from reviewers. *The Telegraph* wrote that 'Byatt struggles to convey these synaptic goings-on [the connections her brain devises between the two artist figures] without condescension' as she puts readers 'firmly in [their] place' ('A. S. Byatt's new book' 2016). However the book, a personal essay written in the first person, offers the Byatt readers an insight into her working mind which prolongs her latest fictional experiments as it is related to her novels from 2009 and 2011, *The Children's Book* and *Ragnarok*.

The connection with *The Children's Book* lies with Fiona McCarthy's biography of artist Eric Gill whose incestuous relations with his daughters inspired the character of Benedict Fludd. *Peacock and Vine* uses Gill's Golden Cockerel typeface which he designed for Golden Cockerel fine press. The careful attention paid by Byatt to her book's typefaces relates, in turn, to *Ragnarok*, where, for the first time, she included a note on the choice of font. Additionally, *Ragnarok* pays homage to a book from Byatt's childhood days, *Asgard and the Gods* adapted from Wagner by M. W. McDowal, and also includes reproductions of print drawings from the original book. Byatt's current focus on the print materiality of the book, which relates to her latest foray in the Arts and Craft movement, points to the agential reality of the book as an object. The object itself is an actor as much as the writer and the reader.

By sharing her sources of inspiration with her readers through the medium of a fine book, Byatt contributes to redistributing our perspective on the world as interrelated networks. Her own thinking mind works through weaving webs of connections. Her recent non-fictional pieces shed light on the changes in her latest fictional writing: they mix together personal anecdotes from her creative life, ekphrases of art works, literary sources of inspiration, the latest scientific discoveries or engineering novelties, social thoughts and behaviours. Thus her 2008 review of a textile exhibition at Compton Verney for *The Guardian*, entitled 'Twisted Yarns', is a reworking of her fictional piece 'Arachne'.

'Arachne' was commissioned in 2000 by Philip Terry and inspired her late French translator Jean-Louis Chevalier to coin the term 'auctorbiography'. In the introduction to the collective book *Ovid Metamorphosed*, Terry described Byatt's text as a 'mixed-genre narrative, weaving together elements of autobiography, essay, art history and sheer storytelling' (2000a: 3). *Ragnarok* and *Peacock and Vine* are similarly mixed-genre narratives depicting the artist as an 'embodied mind' (Byatt 2006) with auctorbiographic insights into the life experiences of the author running alongside her knowledge accretion in a variety of domains. The creative life of A. S. Byatt is permeated with the 'thinginess' (Byatt 2019) of the world that she describes in words. Byatt says she believes in making things (Harrod and Adamson 2011: 81). It is her contention that this new materialism is an answer to both the solipsism inherited from modernism and the ideological inconsistency of postmodern times: 'I think the popularity of craft has to do with my attempt to explain a sort of society that needs craft the more because we have no belief systems. I think we need craft because we need something outside ourselves as people' (Harrod and Adamson 2011: 76).

The notion of an 'embodied mind' originated in Byatt's review of neurologist Antonio Damasio's book *Looking for Spinoza*. Her writing experiments align with the recent interest of posthuman thinking in Spinoza's monistic understanding of the world as one common substance which helps to counter anthropocentrism. For herself, Byatt means to offset narcissism by turning to craft and knowledge: making things, understanding things. Byatt's fictional experiment with omniscience in *The Children's Book* mirrors her goal of painting people as 'incarnate' 'consciousnesses, embedded in the stuff of things' (Byatt 2019) taking her cue from George Eliot and Iris Murdoch. Thus Isobel Armstrong's response to James Wood's heavy-handed criticism of *The Children's Book* on the *London Review of Books*' website underlines the innovative way in which Byatt uses omniscience: 'Wood is right without understanding why when he says that Byatt ignores the tradition of Proust and Woolf: her aim is precisely that, to avoid the open nerve of consciousness. This is not a postmodern novel as Wood suggests, but a major experiment in writing from the outside' (Wood 2009b).

Interestingly enough, Wood condemns Byatt's narratorial voice by exploiting the same arguments as those which he previously used in his famous review of Zadie Smith's *White Teeth*. Just as he reproached Smith's omniscient narrator with giving 'needless little lectures' (2000), so he criticizes Byatt's 'teacherly, qualifying authorial judgement' and calls her an 'authorial examiner' (2009b). Wood is nothing if not consistent in his detestation of what he terms 'a peculiar kind of postmodern 19th century omniscience' (2009b). However, as Armstrong rightly highlights, this voice is not postmodern: it does not offer metafictional comments on the referential illusion and the role of the author–narrator in making up a fiction; instead, it offers observations on the characters themselves, thus reinforcing the reality effect rather than dissolving it. To Wood, who laments the return of realism in contemporary literature and likes to pit it against the classic novels of Dickens and Tolstoy he admires, Smith's omniscient narrator 'not only speaks over her character, she reduces him, obliterates him' (2000). Similarly, he disparages Byatt qualifying her as a good children's writer because she 'talk[s] over her character [which] is what good children's writers do, and do charmingly' (2009b).

In addition to Wood's blatant sexism when he discredits Byatt as a children's writer or when he calls Smith's realism hysterical, his aversion to being lectured, I would argue, is also proportionate to the cultural capital of the two female writers. You need only compare the tone in these two reviews with the much milder one he uses in reviewing the novels of a male realist writer like Ian McEwan. Even though the title of the review is meant to build up the posture of the fierce critique, 'James Wood writes about the manipulations of Ian McEwan' is very much a praise of McEwan's skill which is favourably compared to Tolstoy's. Thus, in the case of McEwan, Wood writes: 'I dislike strong narrative manipulation, but McEwan's Collins-like surprises certainly work. They retain our narrative hunger' (2009a). As opposed to Smith or Byatt then, McEwan is 'a compellingly manipulative novelist'. And while in Smith's case, Wood censures what he thinks of as paranoia – 'There is something essentially paranoid about the belief that everything is connected to everything else' (2000) – with McEwan, he happily agrees to become one of the 'willing, guilty, and finally self-conscious co-conspirators in that machinery of manipulation' (2009a).

Furthermore, while he accords McEwan the benefit of considering his whole oeuvre, he does not favour Byatt with the same courtesy, ignoring the span of her forty-five-year long career. He thus disparages the characteristic ekphrastic art she has developed over the years with the help of one brilliant uncomplimentary sentence: 'the novel quivers in aspic.' He further ignores the goal Byatt set for herself to invest the material dimension of realism to evade egocentricity by stating that, like the pots in the novel, 'characters are similarly described – the life is glazed out of them' (2009b). Similarly he accused Smith of voiding her characters of their human dimension, which he attributes to the overbearing omniscient voice.

But what if the point was precisely to imagine a new conception of the human through a novel distribution of the sensible? Wood is averse to webs and connections, thus he misreads Smith's words from an interview in which she clearly acknowledges that literature crosses over disciplines to better weave together knowledge and affect:

> these are guys [Dave Eggers and David Foster Wallace] who know a great deal about the world. They understand macro-microeconomics, the way the Internet works, math, philosophy, but ... they're still people who know something about the street, about family, love, sex, whatever. That is an incredibly fruitful combination. (Wood 2000)

Byatt and Smith have both opted for realist writing to give a sense of the human reality as embedded in the stuff of the world. Both writers utilize an extra-textual voice to build a community of readers and think out their novels in the making. The writer's voice migrating from the fictional to the non-fictional world prolongs the equality effect of the realist novel: 'this equality [of subject matter in the realist novel] destroys all the hierarchies of representation and also establishes a community of readers as a community without legitimacy, a community formed only by the random circulation of the written word' (Rancière 2011: 14). This random community mirrors the random connections established in the novels which raise the question: what do we have in common? What separates us? Both writers have a similar commitment to engaging with the world in a moral way, hence the regular attacks of the critics about the perceived lecturing voice of the omniscient narrator, which derives from the poststructuralist critique of bourgeois values.

It is no coincidence that both writers cite Iris Murdoch whose conception of art, in both its making and its reception, is analogous to morality in that it promotes empathy towards others. Zadie Smith, in an article published in *The Guardian*, quotes from Murdoch's book of moral philosophy *The Sovereignty of Good*, to expand on the realist novel's capacity to penetrate the consciousnesses of others: 'The chief enemy of excellence in morality (and also in art) is personal fantasy, the tissue of self-aggrandising and consoling wishes and dreams which prevents one from seeing what there is outside one . . .' (2007). From Murdoch's quote on the necessity to evade the ego in order to pay attention to what is outside one's own perception, Smith derives the notion that 'to live well, to write well, you must convince yourself of the inviolable reality of other people' (2007). She calls on readers to similarly strive to understand the author in her own terms and gives examples from her own experience as a reader to make her point: 'I have said that when I open a book I feel the shape of another human being's brain. To me, Nabokov's brain is shaped like a helter-skelter. George Eliot's is like one of those pans for sifting gold. Austen's resembles one of the glass flowers you find in Harvard's Natural History Museum' (2007).

Similarly in a newspaper piece entitled 'Soul Searching', Byatt traces some of what she calls the 'maps of consciousness' of different authors and eras, explaining how George Eliot 'wrote novels informed by her understanding and imagination of the nervous system', how Virginia Woolf's 'myriad of impressions' 'suggests that we cannot see clearly, or outside our own perceptual system', or how Freud mapped out the unconscious spatially. For herself, Byatt claims the influence of neurophysiologist Charles Sherrington, who invented the word 'synapse', and more particularly 'his description of the waking brain (the "head-mass") as "an enchanted loom where millions of flashing shuttles weave a dissolving pattern, always a meaningful pattern though never an abiding one . . ."' (2004b).

Both writers make use of realist omniscience to penetrate the minds of the characters and divine their motivations. They do so to represent embodied moral struggles as Murdoch advised to promote 'a renewed sense of the difficulty and complexity of the moral life and the opacity of persons' (Murdoch 1961: 20). Thus omniscience is not to be viewed as authoritarian omnipotence over the characters' destiny but rather to be thought of as transcendent to the individual consciousness. Approaching, through internal focalization, multiple character casts and commenting, with the voice of omniscience, on their limits, or their blind sides, is to 'think in terms of degrees of freedom, and to picture, in a non-metaphysical, non-totalitarian, and non-religious sense, the transcendence of reality' (Murdoch 1961: 19). Additionally, describing in detail the stuff of our daily lives is also a means to escape the narrowness of the filter of a sole consciousness. This is what Byatt recently repeated about the lesson she learned from Murdoch:

> We saw everything, Murdoch seemed to be suggesting, too easily from inside ourselves. Our sense of value was wound up in our judgement of our own 'sincerity'. In another phrase which I never forgot, which changed the way I looked at things, she wrote, 'For the hard idea of truth we had substituted the facile idea of sincerity.'
>
> You cannot, of course, have a hard idea of truth if you have insufficient faith in the human capacity to apprehend or describe the world. (2019)

She had already underlined that 'the concept of sincerity is "self-centred", the concept of truth "other-centred"' in her essay on Murdoch from 1965, *Degrees of Freedom* (1994b: 5). This capacity to step outside your own shoes is closely related to the reader's activity. In the foreword to *Degrees of Freedom* from 1994, Byatt thus insists that '*Degrees of Freedom* tried to read Iris Murdoch as best it could; and I hope it can be seen, not as a book about my writing, but as a writer's book about writing, a book by a writer reading' (1994b: ix). Barthes denied realism any writerly function because he considered that the third-person narrator dictated the reader's response by controlling the narrative events. Smith and Byatt however write realist novels in order to encourage the reader to step outside of herself and deliberate the reality of other consciousnesses embedded in the larger world.

Furthermore they redefine intertextuality as more than a reader's play with literary codes and structures but as an extension of this capacity for 'unselfing'. I borrow the notion of 'unselfing' from Elaine Scarry whose book *On Beauty and Social Justice* inspired Smith's third novel, *On Beauty*. Scarry also quotes Murdoch to explain that ethical fairness may be reached when experiencing pleasure at a beautiful object that requires us to be in an adjacent position: the reader is not the hero/heroine in the story but takes pleasure in reading the story, the source of that pleasure precisely stems from not being the ego-bound centre of the story. Aesthetic fairness helps promote ethical fairness: 'It is clear that an *ethical fairness* that requires "a symmetry of everyone's relations" will be greatly assisted by an *aesthetic fairness* that creates in all participants a state of delight in their own lateralness' (Scarry 1998: 79). By promoting the writerly, Barthes only decentred the author to place the reader centre stage. By calling both on large casts of characters and on an extensive community of readers, the contemporary realist novel aims to rethink anthropocentrism by considering the agency of books.

The omniscient voice in its extra-textual dimension is instrumental in building up this community of readers that Zadie Smith calls a 'literary republic' (2007). Byatt and Smith make use of the acknowledgement section in their books to draw the lists of books that they used to research their novels. They thus provide their readers with a reading list. In the case of Byatt, her latest two pieces, the novel *Ragnarok* and the essay *Peacock and Vine*, even include bibliographies. Clearly they mean their readers to go beyond the text itself and to go read for themselves. It mirrors their practice of reviewing books for the press. For those two writers, fiction writing and criticism are inextricable from one another: they feed on the news of the world – whether literary, artistic, scientific or sociological – to get inspired for their fiction and to think through what writing novels entails. Thus in the foreword to her essays on Iris Murdoch from 1994, Byatt explains that *'Degrees of Freedom* was first published in 1965, when I had published one novel and was thinking very hard about how to write novels and why I wanted to write them. [...] And I [...] learned a great deal about both writing and thinking' (1994b: viii).

It is both David James's and Vanessa Guignery's contention that Smith's fourth novel, *NW*, was the result of the author's reflections in 'Two Directions for the Novel'. Vanessa Guignery compares Smith's novel with O'Neill's: 'Like Joseph O'Neill's *Netherland*, which Smith reviewed, *NW* may be sitting "at an anxiety crossroads" as the novel both nods towards realism and "retain[s] the wound" inflicted on that narrative mode by the assaults of Joyce and modernism' (2013). David James writes about the 'predictive' relationship between the essay and the novel:

> Indeed *NW* appears unable to figure out what kind of creature to become, the same could be said of *Ulysses*. Smith implied as much four years ago, arguing that 'if literary realism survived the assault of Joyce, it retained the wound.' This assertion – arriving midway through her well-known essay 'Two Directions for the Novel' – is angled as pointedly toward Smith herself as toward those who assume that in fiction today there are no remnants of modernism and that realism reigns unchallenged. It's no coincidence, then, that 'Two Directions for the Novel' owns a strikingly predictive relationship to *NW*. (2013: 205)

Their fiction writing and their essay writing are intricately tangled. A month before the release of her latest novel from 2016, *Swing Time*, Zadie Smith published a piece in *The Guardian* entitled 'Dance Lessons for Writers' which mirrors her preoccupations in the novel. In it she describes major dance figures from all repertoires and divides them along the lines of her quandary with the writerly and the readerly. She distinguishes, for example, Gene Kelly as an 'experimental dancer' from Fred Astaire as a 'grounded' 'transcendent' dancer. She opposes the 'legibility' of Michael Jackson's moves to the 'illegible, private' performances of Prince. She quotes Nabokov again and it is clear the list of dancers arranged in duos repeat the literary division between experimentation and realism.

For the first time in *Swing Time*, Zadie Smith has experimented with a first-person narrator. However she purposely focused the attention on a peripheral character: the first-person narrator is adjacent to her own life; she is the personal assistant of a music star, a disloyal friend and an estranged daughter. She might have yet again taken her cue from Iris Murdoch who, talking about the use of the first person in her novel *The Sea, The Sea*, imagines her ideal novel: 'I've often thought that the best way to write a novel would be to invent the story, and then to remove the hero and the heroine and write about the peripheral people' (Chevalier 1978: 65). Murdoch was talking about the disadvantages of using the first person. Smith, however, wrote a first-person novel dedicated to a peripheral heroine and this is precisely what John Boyne, in his harsh review of the novel, resented the most: 'she's so dull, lacking any discernible wit, intelligence or ambition that she feels less of an independent character and more of an appendage to others, whether friend, daughter or assistant' (2016). Boyne further compares *Swing Time* to Smith's *The Autograph Man* and *NW* on account of what he feels to be a failure in focalization: 'Unfortunately, *Swing Time* joins these two earlier books, lacking a consistent narrative drive, an interesting voice or a compelling point of view' (2016).

By contrast Dayna Tortorici envisages the narrative voice in *Swing Time* as correlated to Smith's extra-textual voice in her essays: 'Smith is one of our best living critics, and she has transposed the instructive, contagious voice of her essays into *Swing Time*. Like Smith the critic, Smith the novelist encourages us to explore what has so enchanted her' (2016). Smith is asking her readers to go through the same experiment she carried out as a writer using the first person: to put themselves in the shoes of a minor character.

As evidenced by Boyne's negative review, Smith, like Byatt, regularly faces forceful attacks from reviewers. As Smith's debate with James

Wood demonstrates, the writers welcome contradiction as a way to deliberate their novel-thinking. Upon the publication of her second collection of essays, *Feel Free*, Smith participated in a question/answer column in *The Guardian* with her readers. She explicitly states that her writing is to be thought of as a dialogue and as a form of thinking:

> I think of myself as thinking about all sorts of things, on the page, in public. I try to point out the idiosyncratic way in which I think and also the commonality I'm seeking. Something like: 'I'm thinking this – are you, reader?' But I don't mind if the answer turns out to be no. I'm less interested in convincing people of an argument than in modelling a style of thinking. (2018)

Byatt enjoys raising polemics in the press. The debate created by her piece for the *New York Times*, 'Harry Potter and the Childish Adult' in 2003, is a paradigmatic example of her reach as a public intellectual figure, as Mariadele Boccardi insists:

> Equally, however, hers is not a voice easily dismissed: the *New York Times* piece provoked a fierce debate in the letters column of the newspaper, with interventions from the general public as well as from fellow-writers in both camps. This reaction to an admittedly provocative piece implicitly acknowledged her influence as a cultural commentator and proved her status as the closest thing to a public intellectual of an Arnoldian, Eliotesque or Leavisite kind in contemporary British literature. (2013: 14)

The problem lies with the heated reactions that, instead of engaging in a dialogue, turn to personal attacks as Hermione Eyre noted in *The Independent*: 'Byatt provoked a torrent of aggressively pro-Potter outrage, some of it phrased as a personal attack. [. . .] And now that this review has led to her being reported as having dropped 'a gobbet of bile' on J. K. Rowling, it seems that she has been flagrantly misread' (2003). Byatt's criticism of Rowling again needs to be read in relation to the Murdoch connection. 'Harry Potter and the Childish Adult' is Byatt's version of 'Against Dryness'. She criticizes Rowling's fiction as escapist, as an example of those crystalline novels that console instead of 'grappl[ing] with reality' (Murdoch 1961: 19). This is the reason why she emphasizes the absence of danger in the books and the caricature of evil, which echoes Murdoch's interrogation about the relative absence of 'convincing pictures of evil' (1961: 20) in modern literature. Harry Potter is anything but opaque, which is why Byatt underlines that, although he is fifteen in *Order of the Phoenix* which she reviews, he still behaves like an eight-year old. And so she questions the adult public's fascination with the books.

This non-fictional piece is closely related to the novel published six years later, *The Children's Book* which precisely displaces the Peter Pan syndrome in the Edwardian period, portraying adults idealizing childhood and manipulating children before the shattering event of the First World War. A year after the Harry Potter review, she published a review of the film *Finding Neverland* for *The Guardian* which mirrors the writer's preoccupations in her novel: 'What happened to the golden boys of the Edwardian Age was, of course, the first world war. "To die will be an awfully big adventure," Peter Pan said blithely on his rock – a line that was cut in performance as the war wore on' (2004b).

In the novel the Wellwood family goes to attend the premiere of the play in 1904. Byatt also came across a historical nugget for her novel: 'researching the novel, she made a discovery that seemed too good – or bad – to be true: soldiers named trenches and redoubts after children's books: "Peter Pan Trench", "Hook Copse", "Wendy Cottage" . . .' (Leith 2009). With the tale of Tom and his shadow, written by his mother Olive, Byatt tells of the dangers of writing real people into fictional stories. Tom's fairy story contrasts with the realistic bullying taking place at the public school he attends and his eventual suicide. Byatt is gesturing towards Harry Potter by reversing the story: instead of the boy stepping into a magic world where the bullied becomes the hero, hers cannot escape reality and his mother's story, especially when the story goes public. While Rowling's books rely on 'the powerful working of the fantasy of escape and empowerment' (Byatt 2003b) for children, Byatt writes of the dangers of fantasy and about death. Indeed by weaving Peter Pan into her novel, she also refers to infantile mortality: 'But Peter Pan, like a lot of dangerous Victorian fantasy, conflates fairyland with death. The Lost Boys are those who vanished from their prams' (Byatt 2004c).

In 2005, Byatt also wrote a review about Lisa Chaney's biography of J. M. Barrie for the *Newstatesman*. The three non-fictional pieces published between 2003 and 2005 are indicative of Byatt's work in progress on *The Children's Book* and of her thinking out her novel in relation to current events and historical research. In addition, June Sturrock has written on how *The Children's Book* should be read in connection with Murdoch's *The Good Apprentice* and shows how Byatt's novel enacts 'Murdoch's ambition of multiple centres' (2010: 124). Sturrock quotes Chevalier's interview with Byatt when Byatt explained 'I did not start as some writers would say they did, with the desire to describe their own lives [. . .]. It is very important to be nobody, rather like the reader inhabiting the book' (Chevalier 1999: 7). Her non-fiction not only references her reading lists when writing a book but also contributes to building a community of readers.

The assiduous writing of non-fictional pieces by the two writers testifies to a long-standing debate on realism and the novel that, far from being exhausted, is being revived by the current interrogations on the perception of reality as being composed of a diversity of non-human agencies, including books. Both Byatt and Smith refigure the role of the contemporary writer as a public intellectual figure whose extra-textual voice in newspaper columns prolongs that of omniscience in the fictional world. By doing so they also redefine the reader's compact in an exigent way, as Smith wrote: 'Read better.' They are taking an ethical stand both in relation to their characters and their readers by affirming the value of complex debates that are sorely needed today in democracies around the world. Opting for realism despite its criticisms is an even more committed choice as they are women, meaning that they are still expected to answer for their ambitions. The redefinition of the writer's voice in relation to the reading compact on the basis of weaving together thoughts and feelings also opens up new possibilities for realist characterization, which the next chapter will investigate.

3

Abjection, self-abjection and social mutations

Engaging with the reader

Prolonging the redefinition of the reading compact, the use of abjection in contemporary realist novels is meant to actively engage the reader in an affective dialogue with the text.

Abjection theory was originally outlined by Julia Kristeva based on her reading of Mikhail Bakhtin's grotesque theory (see Vice 1997). In *Powers of Horror*, she uses the same categories as Bakhtin's – bodily borders, maternity, food and death – to deliver a psychoanalytical analysis of subject formation. Kristeva uses Lacan's distinction between the three orders of the imaginary, the symbolic and the real. She focuses especially on the symbolic which regulates the subject's sociality through language. According to Kristeva, access to the symbolic order of language and the symbolic apprehension of one's own body is based on the rejection of the maternal body which represents indistinct fusion. To recognize the boundaries of one's proper body, one needs to abjectify its orifices: the mouth, the eyes, the ears, the anus and the female sex undermine the clear-cut distinction between the inner and the outer. The seepage of substances through those orifices also attests to the porosity between the inside and the outside. This is how Kristeva accounts for the disgusted feelings associated with faeces and for the prohibition related to menses. A subject's social relations are thus determined by an ordered view of the body and its related prohibitions as well as by the dividing line of sexual difference.

This is the reason why Kristeva's abjection theory inspired the feminist analyses of the grotesque. The ambivalence of the female grotesque body, emblematized by Bakhtin's reference to the figure of the pregnant hag, represents a threat to the symbolic order. In feminist art, it can thus be used transgressively to highlight the social exclusion of queer bodies and to spectacularize deviant female identities (see Russo 1995). Magic realist or fantastic writings have been singled out as the archetypal tool to effect those extraordinary metamorphoses in correlation with the view that realism stands for the norm. Russo uses the now paradigmatic example of the bird-woman Fevvers in Angela Carter's *Nights at the Circus*. Carter's character further relates to the founding text by Hélène Cixous, 'The Laugh of the Medusa', which urges women to escape the phallic symbolic order by writing 'female-sexed texts' (1976: 877). Fevvers who sports queer avian appendages and who cooks up tall tales is a literary embodiment of Cixous's 'femme qui vole', or flying/stealing women: 'women take after birds and robbers [. . .] They (*illes*) go by, fly the coop, take pleasure in jumbling the order of space, in disorienting it, in changing around the furniture, dislocating things and values, breaking them all up, emptying structures, and turning propriety upside down' (Cixous 1976: 887).

The classic realist text, with its ordered descriptions of furniture – let's just have in mind the opening pages of *Eugénie Grandet* – may seem at first to not be the proper choice to 'dislocate things and values'. However, as Rancière outlined, the redistribution of perception it effected disrupted the hierarchies of Aristotelean representation, in particular the choice of common people as main characters, which became the standard of realism. Contemporary realist novels reconnect with the initial democratic gesture of realism.

Contemporary realist novels by women writers add a further abject dimension to their characters' self-perception which relates to the feminist revolution that uncovered internalized self-loathing in female subject formation.

Rose Tremain and Pat Barker opt for a naturalist approach to portrait-making in realist fiction. They purposely delve into their characters' filthy minds, repeat words from their foul mouths and expose the environmental factors that shape deviant personalities. They have appropriated and revised Hippolyte Taine's famous explanation of naturalist thought as taking into account 'race, milieu and moment' in its portrayal of outcasts; in other words, heredity, social environment and history. The feminist inquiry into the history of social prohibitions, its basis in psychoanalytical analyses of the speaking subject and its family history, and its criticism of scientific discourse in the power games of patriarchal society, have modified the original nineteenth-century approach to naturalist depiction. As Mark Rawlinson underlines, one major trait of this modification belongs with the reader who is no longer a spectator but is invited to experience the characters' self-perception:

> Barker's working-class novels have been criticized for their affinity with nineteenth-century naturalism (which means above all the novelist strategies of Zola), that is for the way the observing narrator fixes the characters in terms of 'physical and manual' detail, from the point of view of an objectifying observer: thus *Union Street* has been described as '*about* the working class, not of it' (Dodd and Dodd, 122–4). But this reading underestimates the extent to which Barker was already endeavouring to make us experience events, rather than have us mere spectators, and this concern is a key motivation of her developing narratorial style. (2010: 46–7)

This aligns with the remarks from the previous chapter about revised omniscience. Women writers contest the detachment of the observer constructed by Western phallocentric science by engaging the reader in an affective empirical experience. This experience does not necessarily rely on empathy: Pat Barker, Andrea Levy and Rose Tremain rehabilitate the scandalous nature of realism by imagining nasty characters who raise feelings of antipathy in the reader. The strategies differ from one novel to the next: they experiment with narratorial style to investigate the variety of reading compacts in relation to abjection.

Tremain's novels are populated with abject characters with criminal backgrounds: murderers, rapists, paedophiles, collaborationists. When constructing antipathetic characters, Tremain usually relies on what Georges Letissier has called 'neo-characterization': she imports character types from past novels that she reworks in a contemporary environment. This strategy allows the reader to measure the gap between past social relations and current mutations. This interrogation systematically aligns with the dividing line between the sexes.

In her first novel from 1976, *Sadler's Birthday*, Tremain was bold enough to opt for a paedophile figure as her main character, the butler Sadler. The novel, narrating the butler's reminiscences of the Second World War, anticipated Kazuo Ishiguro's Booker-prize winning *The Remains of the Day*. As in Ishiguro's novel, the butler stands for an archaic yet persistent British class system. Tremain's novel however renews the genre of the *bildungsroman* by reversing the prototypical Dickensian plot of the underdog maturing into a socially fit adult. The novel references Dickens's novels, *Great Expectations* and *Little Dorrit*. Sadler is an orphan-turned-butler who comes to inherit, in his old age, the house of his late masters. Reminiscing about his one and only love story when he engaged in an inappropriate relationship with a boy evacuee housed in the manor, Sadler stands for a figure of infantile attachment. He cherishes the memory of his mother and displays a fierce detestation of women. The extended comparison running through the novel between Sadler and his dog abjectifies the underdog figure. Sadler's obsession with his past queers him into a contemporary male version of Miss Havisham. This is achieved through third-person internal focalization.

Tremain later turned to polyphony. Her fourth novel from 1985, *The Swimming Pool Season*, pays homage to Balzac's *Comédie humaine* and to Zola's *L'Assomoir*. She neo-characterizes Zola's character, Gervaise, to give her a new destiny. In Zola's nineteenth-century Paris, Gervaise was exploited by turn-coat Lantier and crippled drunk Coupeau. In Tremain's contemporary rural France, Gervaise chooses a ménage à trois by taking a German lover, Klaus, to bear the burden of her unemployed misogynist and Pétainist husband, Mallélou. The hereditary traits that affected Gervaise in Zola's novel, her limp and her alcoholism, are transferred onto the male characters in crisis in Tremain's novel. Mallélou is a drunk while the village's doctor, Hervé, a phallocrat bachelor, is crippled by a fall like Coupeau. Tremain depicts masculine crisis through burdening her male characters with physical impairments and afflictions.

Her eleventh novel from 2010, *Trespass*, rewrites the character type of the femme fatale while paying homage to Claude Chabrol, the representative of naturalism in the French cinema, who followed in the footsteps of Jean Renoir:

> 'You're too young to have seen *Le Boucher* by Claude Chabrol,' Tremain says. 'It's a devastatingly good film, quite horrendous.' *Trespass* begins with a homage to a scene from that film, about a serial killer in a small French village. 'A teacher takes her kids on a picnic,' Tremain continues. 'There is an overhanging cliff, a close-up of a girl's hand on a baguette, and blood starts to drip on to it. I wanted to find in my book a moment of terror as powerful as that. My working title, which my New York agent said was pulpy and camp, was Blood Sandwich'. (Tremain 2010)

The murderer in Tremain's novel is an old woman, Audrun, who kills an Englishman who has come to buy her property in the Cévennes region of France. Audrun was abused in her teenage years by her father and her brother, Aramon, who also cruelly tarnished her mother's memory by having Audrun believe she was the daughter of a German invader. The novel thus references the historical origin of *noir* invented by André Breton whose *Anthologie de l'humour noir*, first published in 1939, was censored by the Vichy government and only started to circulate after 1945. In 1945, Marcel Duhamel founded the publishing imprint 'Série noire' for Gallimard, a collection of crime fiction and American hard-boiled detective novels. Both Breton's term and the Gallimard collection served as the basis for the development of the cinematic concept of *noir*. Playfully imagining the perfect murder, Tremain neo-characterizes the stock character of *noir*, the femme fatale, by drawing on the social invisibility of old women while writing in the black humour vein of Breton. As one reviewer remarked, 'none of the characters in "Trespass" are likable. On the contrary, to a one, they are self-interested, embittered and vindictive. At times, Tremain's exposures, always merciless, verge on the assaultive' (Leavitt 2010). Tremain rewrites atavistic family stories in parallel with the darkest hours of European history through a foray into her characters' psychopathology.

Pat Barker, too, writes in a naturalist vein and does not hesitate to tackle the abject. Her work reconnects with the classic realists' inspiration drawn from famous crime cases narrated in the tabloids. In Zola's *La Bête humaine*, the son of Gervaise turns out to be a serial killer whom Zola called Jacques in reference to Jack the Ripper. Barker's second novel, *Blow Your House Down*, was famously inspired by the serial murders of Peter Sutcliffe who was dubbed the Yorkshire Ripper. Her ninth novel, *Border Crossing*, was inspired by the murder case of James Patrick Bugler and raises the issue of young offenders.

In her first novel, *Union Street*, one of the objects circulating in the different chapters is the tabloid *News of the World*. It first appears on the kitchen table on Sunday in Kelly Brown's chapter. It is read by Liza at the maternity ward while she recalls the doctor's refusal to give her an abortion. It most pathetically covers the body of Brenda's infant son left to die on the bathroom floor by her mother Iris King after a failed attempt at abortion. Like Iris herself, strolling down the chapters as she does the street's houses, the newspaper makes its way into the various households. It is a 'material-semiotic node' (Harraway 1991: 200) whose physical, occasional yet persistent presence encodes Barker's denotation of 'small worlds' that 'connote [. . .] larger worlds' (Rawlinson 2010: 13). It is an illustration of how Barker dramatizes the anecdotal by giving it a new emphasis: the newspaper is commonly referred to as sensational but Barker, by incarnating those sensational stories, uncovers the actual scandalous nature of those small ordinary dramas. Thus what is revealed as truly shocking is that, for the women of Union Street, those stories are but habitual. The violence of having to deal with the consequences of foreseen or unforeseen pregnancy is but routine; it never makes the front page except when it can be aggrandized to feed the public's appetite for horrifying stories. By depicting the minuscule lives of undervalued people, Barker reconnects with the initial democratic gesture of realism described by Jacques Rancière, and with the novelist's role characterized by Edmond de Goncourt, Zola's friend, in his 1888 preface to *La Faustin* as that of 'a historian of those who have no history'.

Mark Rawlinson argues that Barker's pornographic writing in *Blow Your House Down*, understood as 'writing about prostitutes', precisely serves the function of 'an extended counter-statement, a voicing of what is silenced, and a scrupulous revision of a dismissive or exploitative misrepresentation of prostitutes' (2010: 32). As is well known, Barker attended a writing class with Angela Carter. Thus her pornographic writing can be likened to Carter's polemical definition of Sade as a 'moral pornographer' in *The Sadeian Woman*. Carter argued that the moral pornographer is an artist who 'might use pornography as a critique of the current relations between the sexes' (2009: 22). The highly controversial scene of the murder of Kath as told from the point of view of the killer renders the abjectification of the woman's flesh. Ann Ardis takes up the distinction established by Hortense Spillers about Black slaves to account for the shocking description of Kath's corpse. Kath's is no longer a gendered body, that could still be read along the lines of an iconography of sexual difference, but lifeless flesh, objectified and abjectified, ungendered. Pornography turns to morality as the reader is shocked into experiencing 'awareness of our capacity to turn subjectivity into property, bodies into flesh' (Ardis 1991: 53).

Tremain's neo-Victorian novel from 2003, *The Colour*, also tackles prostitution. Through child prostitution in the gold mines of New Zealand, Tremain dramatizes her character's pathological scare of women. Joseph Blackstone is an amateur of anal rape because he fears pregnancy. He flees England after the murder of his girlfriend in a failed attempt at abortion. He settles in New Zealand having conveniently married a governess but their marriage remains unconsummated. Instead Joseph pays a male child prostitute for intercourse. Tremain uses Thomas Hardy's technique of landscape depiction to dramatize the couple's rift: the New Zealand landscape expresses the characters' feelings. David James tells of the phenomenological approach to landscape depiction: 'She certainly extends Thomas Hardy's ambition to engage phenomenologically with places rather than reduce them to topographical labelling' (2008: 8). Thus when Joseph descries the female figures of his wife and of his mother on a hill, his feeling of oppression relates to his misogynous fear of women:

> Joseph understood that his will was cramped by the near presence of his wife and his mother. He dreaded to see either of them there, walking towards him, with the wind billowing their skirts. He went so far as to feel that the very shape of a woman on a hillside appeared to him now as an ugly and oppressive thing. (Tremain 2004: 75)

The revised Impressionistic tableau, ironically recalling Monet's *Femme à l'ombrelle tournée vers la gauche*, translates the character's abjection. The ravaged earth of the gold mines and 'the oozing mud of the river-bottom' (2004: 185) similarly transcribe the daily anal rape of the child prostitute. Tremain's feminist perspective uses omniscient narration to develop a material–semiotic connection between physical space and mental space, as well as between feeling and thinking: 'Tremain's own focalized way of describing place complements this intersection between feeling and thought – formally as well as dramatically' (James 2008: 9).

Moral pornography in contemporary naturalist novels calls on the reader's various affects in relation to abjection to raise awareness of moral issues involved in focalization as both a writing and a reading experience. Thus Ardis's paper on her class's responses to Barker's novel insists on the way the text 'calls attention to the voyeurism involved in any reading experience, particularly when reading involves identification across lines of social classifications' (1991: 49). The seriality of murders in famous crime cases also finds a strange echo in the serial format of publication of the great realist novels by Balzac, Zola or Dickens. The murdering impulse of serial killers who cannot stop themselves, as dramatized by Zola in *La Bête humaine*, echoes the reading impulse as addicted to knowing what comes next. However contemporary naturalist texts by women writers problematize those impulses by holding a mirror to the reader through strategies of focalization calling into question their affective response that can be either negative or positive. One could argue that Barker's favourite mode of sequel writing, which she most famously used with the *Regeneration* trilogy and later with the *Life Class* trilogy, allows the readers to develop an extended affective relationship with the recurring characters. This is also the case with one of Rose Tremain's most engaging characters, Merivel, who first appeared in *Restoration* in 1989 and was the subject of a sequel thirteen years later in *Merivel: A Man of His Time*. Another sympathetic character, Ruby Constad, the first-person narrator of her second novel *Letter to Sister Benedicta* from 1978, reappeared in 2008 in *The Road Home*.

Those two first-person narrators from Tremain's novels share a similar trait: their narrative is marked by self-abjection. Both characters draw depreciative self-portraits. Ruby describes herself as a 'Nuisance' with the capital N highlighting the major inconvenience she imagines herself to have become. Now that her children have left home and that her husband suffered a stroke, Ruby feels redundant: she feels she has outlived her usefulness as a mother and a housewife. She depicts herself as 'a big snail, lumbering round the corners of his [her husband's] life [. . .] I have moved so slowly, got in everybody's way. I have been huge and purposeless' (1999a: 53). Merivel, from the novel's incipit, warns the reader of his many flaws: 'I am an affront to neatness. [. . .] I am erratic, immoderate, greedy, boastful and sad' (2009: 3). He then narrates his career as Charles II's fool and later as a knave doctor during the Plague outbreak. In addition, both narrators are confessional writers. Ruby is writing a journal/letter addressed to a nun at the Indian convent where she spent her childhood. Merivel is writing his memoir inspired by the journal of Samuel Pepys which exposed 'his own self-mockery and touching honesty about his worldly striving' (Tremain 2013).

The reader as addressee has a crucial role to play as a symbolic agent in the reconstruction of the characters' identity through narration. Both characters try to make sense of their life experiences with the help of the reader. The comic tone adopted in the two self-deprecating confessions is meant to win the reader's sympathy so that the reader is instrumental in according Ruby the recognition of herself as a person of note and Merivel the redemption he is looking for. Instead of the classic realist readers being but supposedly manipulated into a consensual moral judgement of a character's fate, they are called upon as agents who are free to lend help or not to the characters depending on whether they were moved by their narrative. The reviews, as records of readers' responses, are useful in that light. Merivel is largely considered as sympathetic. He is the figure of the 'lovable rogue' (Daniel 2012). In the sequel to *Restoration*, Richard Eder however found that 'as a character he falls just a little short of compelling' (2013). Reviewers indeed do not hesitate to evaluate books in relation to the affect they experienced in their relationship with the characters. It is a preeminent characteristic of Tremain's reception and has been outlined by Sue Sorensen as the writer's true inventiveness: 'ambitious and risk-taking in her characters and events, she is less experimental in language and structure than many of her contemporaries'. Why would characterization be considered any less a field for experimentation than language though?

Rita Felski sums up the joint legacy of Lacan's and Althusser's theories of misrecognition in the poststructuralist reception of realism as misleading the reader with a false notion of the self as unified:

> Whether the work of fiction is analogous to the mirror or the police, it seeks to lull readers into a misapprehension of their existence as unified, autonomous individuals. Storytelling and the aesthetics of realism are deeply implicated in this process of misrecognition because identifying with characters is a key mechanism through which we are drawn into believing in the essential reality of persons. (2008: 28)

This is the basis of Kristeva's abjection theory: the subject needs to abjectify the imaginary narcissistic relationship to its mother to enter the symbolic realm of language. Thus subverting the feminine abject in French feminist theory means upsetting the phallic symbolic order. However, by relocating abjection in the imaginary self of her characters and the imaginary identification of her readers, Tremain reconnects with the notion of the symbolic as a complex network of intersubjective relations. Those relations are not only ones of ideological entrapment, narcissistic seducement or gullible delusion but also of difficult truths and mutual self-help. That readers are positioned as the representatives of the symbolic order gives them a responsibility towards the characters and encourages them to question their own affect. As Felski reminds us, fiction is not simply a seductive lie:

> The Lacanian picture of the child gazing entranced at its own idealized self-image thus falls notably short as a schema for capturing how literature represents selves. The experience of reading is often akin to seeing an unattractive, scowling, middle-aged person coming into a restaurant, only to suddenly realize that you have been looking into a mirror behind the counter and that this unappealing-looking person is you. Mirrors do not always flatter; they can take us off guard, pull us up short, reflect our image in unexpected ways and from unfamiliar angles. [. . .] We can value literary works precisely because they force us – in often unforgiving ways – to confront our failings and blind spots rather than shoring up self-esteem. (2008: 48)

Andrea Levy's *Small Island* also uses affective focalization to expose racism by exhibiting its abjectifying process. Her two Black first-person narrators, Hortense and Gilbert, display an overly proper language whose civility lays bare the rudeness of the Mother Country. The highly decorous English they have learned matches the idealistic picture of the British Empire they belong to which comes undone when they set foot in England where the English do not understand what they are saying and cannot place Jamaica on a map. Hortense's wish to conform makes her an antipathetic snobbish character, thus upending rectitude as a positive value. Because etiquette turns out to parade unbelonging, it, in fact, uncovers the repressed abject foundation of the empire: the commodification of the Jamaican people alongside the colonial products covered over by the honourable discourse of the benevolent motherland. Hortense's narrative is characterized by repeated misunderstandings that comically portray the English as impolite, if not downright illiterate in their own language, reversing the colonial racist bias on the uncivilized savages. Ideality and propriety clash with the reality of bullying and prejudices. The Jamaican story of Hortense heralds her disastrous English experience: just as she betrays first her surrogate brother and then her best friend for opportunistic reasons, stealing away their lovers, so she is betrayed in turn by the idolized empire that would rather keep her away from sight on her small Caribbean island. The cultural clash is materialized geographically by the diasporic transition. It occurs when the Jamaican characters realize that, on English soil, they are not considered as English whereas the colonial internalized notion of racial difference characterizes social space in Jamaica: Hortense believes at first that her lighter skin shade will offer her opportunities. Focalization thus takes on another dimension in Levy's by confronting the readers with the symbolic construction of racist bias.

Racial difference is further complicated by sexual difference in the novel as the female characters struggle with the return of patriarchal values that the war had capsized. Thus both Hortense and Queenie have to cope with husbands they initially elected as their sole escape from a fated female destiny: Queenie to escape the family butchery, Hortense to escape her lack of prospects in Jamaica. Both are disgusted by having sex with their husbands. Queenie's depiction of marital sex echoes with hints at marital rape as it does not matter to Bernard whether she is aroused: 'Slippery as a greasy sausage sometimes but mostly it was the bark of a tree' (2009: 215). Hortense refuses sex altogether horrified at the sight of 'this hideous predicament between his legs' (2009: 86), 'his disgustingness' (2009: 87). Abjectified maleness reverses the cultural abjection of the female sex, thus exposing the predicament of women whose sole prospect is marriage which, like colonial rule, covers over sexual commodification with a gallant discourse of courtship and the metaphor of the nation as a well-ordered household. Although not cast in the naturalist tradition, Levy's realism also does upset the hierarchy of imperial and patriarchal values that the Second World War shattered as indicated by the novel's structural split of the four narratives between 'Before' and '1948'. The transitional temporal marker echoes the geographic passage of the Windrush generation.

Furthermore, as Corinne Duboin has observed, the relegation of Bernard Bligh's narrative at the end of the novel 'tall[ies] with the author's intentional decentering of a once predominant white male discourse' (2011: 30). Bernard Bligh, who sees himself as the epitome of British masculinity, is first characterized by Queenie as physically abject: she is disgusted with the back of his neck and the worm-like vein in his temple (2009: 210), his kiss with 'puckered lips' feels like 'a chicken's beak' (2009: 211). In her eyes, he is both feminized and infantilized, thus portraying him unfavourably in comparison to the times' standards of ideal masculinity: he looks 'queer' (2009: 210) and when Queenie tries to break up with him, he cries 'like a baby' (2009: 212). He is then portrayed as cowardly, hiding away in the shelter, and enrolling late in the war. Upon finally reading his first-person account, the reader is confronted with a delusional character who thinks he knows better but is systematically proven wrong by his comrades. The text materializes Bernard's self-deception of seniority and superiority with the use of parenthetical asides that manifest his conceited sense of supremacy. The scene of rape of a child prostitute before he finally leaves India again exposes the abject bedrock of colonialism all the more so as Bernard obstinately asserts that he is 'proud to be part of the British Empire. Proud to represent decency' (2009: 311).

By confronting abject self-images and personalities, contemporary realism reaffirms its initial scandalous nature. Jacques Rancière has analysed this scandal as introducing a disturbance in the hierarchy of subjects enforced by the classic epic model. Pat Barker's latest novel, *The Silence of the Girls*, that rewrites the Iliad, characterizes the clash between realism and the epic by contrasting the heroic narrative of Achilles with the first-person narrative of captive Briseis. In an interview, Barker has explicitly related the contestation of the epic with the female perspective:

> The epic is, fundamentally, a very hostile environment for women; the lives of women are not epic in that sense. So as soon as you foreground women you're more or less bound to start questioning the epic form and as soon as you question the epic form, you have a way to bring women into the narrative. (Greengrass 2018)

Briseis's narrative depicts the brutal pornography of the war while her first-person utterance recalls that of Jean in *Blow Your House Down*: the captive women become slaves, the properties of the victors who are used for sex. The captives' dialogue in chapter 6 relates the sexual preferences of their owners and exposes the brutal treatment of Chryseis whom Agamemnon likes to sodomize. It recalls the prostitutes' customary meeting at the pub in the opening scene of *Blow Your House Down*. Claire Armitstead has compared the dialogue with pub gossip:

> Though the story hasn't been updated in any overt way, her Greek and Trojan women are gossiping all around us in the homely north of England pub. As she says of her characters: 'They are very north-eastern – and why not? It's about toughness, irreverence, humour and bitterness all thrown in together'. (2019a)

It is precisely the migration of north-eastern traits in the Trojan context that has puzzled many reviewers who do not hesitate to speak of anachronisms because they are used to read Barker as a historical novelist. Sophie Gilbert is irritated with the language used by Barker: 'Barker also includes anachronisms that can be jarring. Achilles is teased that he's gained weight, as much as "half a stone." When he claims Briseis as his property, he does so by saying, "Cheers, lads. She'll do"' (2018). The inadequacy of measuring units and time markers leads Emily Wilson to question the credibility of Briseis's voice:

> The novel has some anachronisms, such as a 'weekend market' (there were no weekends in antiquity), and a reference to 'half a crown', as if we were in the same period as Barker's first world war novels. One wonders if any woman in archaic Greece, even a former queen, would have quite the self-assurance of Barker's Briseis. (2018)

Geraldine Brooks has delivered a harsh review of Barker's novel once again making a parallel between narrative incongruities and Briseis's voice deemed to be inauthentic:

> I began to lose faith on the first page of the novel when Briseis describes the retreat of the Lyrnessus women and children, hastening from their homes to seek refuge in the citadel: 'Like all respectable married women, I rarely left my house – although admittedly in my case the house was a palace – so to be walking down the street in broad daylight felt like a holiday.' The jarring inauthenticity of this sentence is sadly characteristic of the novel as a whole. It's implausible that a Bronze Age woman in a besieged city would be enjoying a stroll as she hears 'shouts, cries, the clash of sword on shields' just on the other side of the city gates and knows that her husband and brothers are out there, fighting for their lives. (2018)

As attested by those reviews, the scandal of Barker's rewriting of Greek mythology is a direct consequence of the realist mode of her writing. It goes to show the poststructuralist misapprehension of the 'reality effect', as Barker is reproached with a lack of verisimilitude and authenticity, while, in fact, her text produces an 'equality effect': the Greek queen Briseis talks the same way as a prostitute from northern England. Realism indeed erodes the proprieties of the epic. Barker herself said that 'all the anachronisms are deliberate' (Armitstead 2019a). The diegetic anachronisms repeat and signal the impropriety of the narrative voice. Indeed Briseis's voice is scandalous as the epic would not allow a female slave to speak. The wrongness of the time references talks to the wrongness of Briseis speaking. Briseis's speech is purposely malapropos: it is out-of-time and out-of-place. Realism breaks down the rules of epic propriety just as, by speaking, Briseis upsets the rules of property: 'A slave isn't a person who's being treated as a thing. A slave *is* a thing' (Barker 2018: 38).

It is a recurrent question in Barker's work and one that Merritt Moseley addresses by suggesting that although critics have tackled the issue of Barker's realism, 'there remain at least two areas that deserve a clarifying treatment' (2008: 132). One of them is precisely 'her use of the "real" past' (Moseley 2008: 132) as critics like to point out historical inconsistencies in historical novels. *The Silence of the Girls* clarifies this issue by not being a historical novel, as Barker herself highlighted in answer to the anachronism debate:

> Her soldiers are prone to breaking out in bawdy ballads when drunk, 'and I keep having to explain that I don't exactly believe that Homeric warriors were singing English rugby songs either'. What, she asks, does it mean to say a character who never existed was anachronistic? 'You can be anachronistic about Elizabeth I but not about Helen.' (Armitstead 2019a)

The other area that Moseley feels needs to be clarified is whether or not Barker's novels are postmodern. It is my contention that disentangling ourselves from the constructionist perspective and adopting an *avant-gardiste* view of realism as the bastard genre it was always designed to be, helps clear up the issue. Barker's novels, like Tremain's, do not display postmodernist features. They are naturalist novels being reinvented with the help of feminism. They display in particular the harshness of the divisions between the sexes. The use of slang, gesturing towards the classic naturalist novel which shocked the conservative readers of the time with its coarse language, is adopted to transcribe the abuse of women.

Pat Barker's *Union Street* displays the variety of slang words for the female sex: fanny, cunt, tash, crack. Most strikingly, the words are used by the women themselves making it clear that they have been disciplined to despise and hate their own sex. Kelly Brown fears to grow up and display signs of femaleness like her sister, the slang word echoes her disgust: 'no, she didn't want to get like that. And she certainly didn't want to drip foul-smelling, brown blood out of her fanny every month' (1999: 11). When she defiles the headmaster's office in a fit of rage, she writes on the board 'the worst word she knew: CUNT' (1999: 57). When Lisa is in hospital having delivered a baby girl, the women joke about how baby girls are not wanted: 'Don't bring it round here if it's got a crack in it' (1999: 126). It contrasts with the sanitized word 'vagina' used by the doctor upon his examination of Lisa's cervix. The reader is meant to experience what it is like to be a woman with a curse.

Similarly, Levy uses the many racist words used in England at the time to debase Black and Indian people: nigger, wog, gollywog, blackie, coolie. They echo the episodes that expose the racist bullying and humiliation experienced by Gilbert: he is threatened by GIs for having tea with Queenie at a teashop, and then for going to the pictures with her and her father-in-law Arthur, which results dramatically in the death of Arthur. Gilbert is demoted at his job by a new colleague who refuses to work with him and is then bullied at a warehouse while retrieving the post. When Bernard finally comes home and finds out that Queenie has taken Gilbert as a lodger, he verbally abuses Gilbert. While exposing the crude reality of xenophobic hatred, Levy skilfully uses the comic to alleviate the racist violence of the episodes by contrasting them with Hortense's naïve perspective that turns racist bias against itself when portraying the uncouth English.

Another of Tremain's confessional first-person writers opts for a different strategy by turning opprobrium into a eulogy of debasement through assaultive comic writing. In *Music and Silence*, Kirsten Munk, the morganatic bride of the king of Denmark Christian IV, writes a diary. She unburdens herself of her frustrations with her sexed predicament through an aggressively comic writing. Kirsten is fed up with her husband's kind but demeaning treatment and opts for self-debasement: 'I no longer have the desire to be a "mousie" [the King's surname for Kirsten]. I would prefer to be a rat. Rats have sharp teeth that will bite. Rats carry disease that will kill. Why do husbands refuse to understand that we women do not for long remain their Pet creatures?' (2000: 8). She will avenge herself on other women whom she treats like her pets and on the Black slaves she exploits sexually. She explicitly states her hatred of children and likes to imagine herself as an empowered woman at war with men: 'Were I a Real Queen, I declare I would occupy some strategically Placed Castle and, from its safety, fire cannonballs at each and every Man who attempted to come near me! And I do not jest. I declare I do despise them all' (2000: 106). To defy her husband, she takes a lover with whom she engages in SM relations and exchanges insults:

> Our Flayings and Whippings are now refined and perfected into Absolute Lust by the means of Words. I do not dare to set down what Insults we have screamed out to each other, only to record that if Otto accuses of being 'a verit. Wh. & strump., a fornic. troll . . . etc. etc. . . .' these terms are quite habitual, even mild and courteous, and we are gone so far into Abuse of each other's Names that I do declare we need some Dictionary to help us come by some new terms that have not been staled with use. (2000: 86)

She ends up being exiled from the court and delights in the name calling of which she is the object: 'it is possible to imagine that the very name Kirsten has become a Forbidden Word in Copenhagen and that those who wish to speak of me must dream up some new Terms for me, such as "The Grand Adulteress" or "The Rhenish Count's Whore" or "She Who Fled Away in the Fish Cart"' (2000: 207). Kirsten turns self-humiliation into self-empowerment through comic writing. She is at war with the king and at war with male dominance and bombards the reader with her rages. As with Ruby and Merivel, the comic appropriation of self-debasement helps foster the reader's sympathy towards the character. The readers are called upon to compensate Kirsten's ostracism by recognizing the validity of her outrage: she is a woman 'driven insane with carrying children' (2000: 57) and with submitting to a phallocentric system.

Abjection and self-abjection problematize social mutations regarding gender relations. As Christine Harrison points out, the masculine attitude of Kirsten and the feminized identity of Merivel and the cavaliers demonstrate that 'Tremain's novels always represent transgender identities within the context of particular social relations' (2012: 232). The protagonist of *Sacred Country* is an FTM transsexual, which makes sense in Tremain's overall experiment with gender mutations. Tremain depicts a masculinity in crisis whose feminization transcribes the characters' feeling of vulnerability, often in the context of the workplace: in *The Swimming Pool Season*, Larry loses his job and becomes feminized in the eyes of his wife while Mallélou's unemployment turns him into a caricature of misogyny. In *The Road Home*, the Eastern European migrant Lev is feminized by his experiences of ostracism. Conversely, women characters are often complicit with the very system that confines them to minor roles. Lev's compatriot, Lydia, experiences downward social mobility when migrating to England and, in the end, resigns herself to become the mistress of a famous conductor.

The reader has an essential role to play in according the minor characters a recognition that society refuses them. By becoming a symbolic agent, the reader may enact alternative solidarities that would promote different social models:

> Like many other new historical novels, Tremain's *Restoration* and *Music and Silence* facilitate similar imaginative crossings between a wide range of gender and sexuality identities. [. . .] these novels highlight the enabling features of past imaginings. One of these features is the conception of plans that may well be within the readers' powers '*if only they dare*' (Harrison 2012: 236)

Similarly, while Barker's novels offer a bleak outlook on society, the reading activity is meant as an act of reparation of the rifts in the neighbourhoods, the life of the country, the life of people. In *Union Street*, the reader is positioned as a neighbour visiting the chapters as Iris does the houses. In addition, the reader is meant to spot the objects that Barker's 'omnipresent voice' (Brannigan 2005a: 30) scatters through the chapters like bread crumbs. They are material–semiotic nodes that trace a precarious, anecdotal thread between the chapters like the tabloid News of the World, or the conkers. In Kelly Brown's chapter, the green conkers she collects figure the young girl's rape when the rapist inserts his fingers in their immature casing: 'She watched his long fingers with their curved nails probe the green skin, searching for the place where it would most easily open and admit them' (1999: 20). They next appear in Joanne Wilson's chapter when her lover takes her under a tree in the park: Joanne is pregnant and fears to share the same fate as exhausted Lisa Goddard who is the subject of the next chapter. Thus the slight insignificant objects are meant to bear meaning and reflect the dramatic way the life experiences of those women are customarily trivialized.

By reconstructing the various narratives as one, the reader plays a role in acknowledging the meaningfulness of trivia, the significance of commonality in the dramatic context of ordinary violence. This is what Elizabeth Ward calls the 'life-sustaining elements' of the novel, in particular 'its recurring use of the natural world as a metaphor of grace' (1983) like the tree that recurs in the opening and closing chapters. They express the synecdochic thread between the human body and the non-human bodies, the human lifespan and the seasons, life and death: 'There are many more such images, which suggest the fragility of protective shells such as body and home, and serve to identify the women symbolically with each other' (Brannigan 2005a: 24).

The reader is called upon not so much as a co-producer of the text as in Barthes's theory but as a companion to the characters. The reader may be exemplified by the major figure of the analyst Rivers in the *Regeneration* trilogy. Karolyn Steffens proposes to contrast Rivers's view of the talking cure with Freud's in order to highlight Barker's practice of realist writing without referring to poststructuralism, thereby clarifying the issue exposed by Merritt Moseley:

> While critics cite Barker's intertextuality and tropes of haunting to fit her into poststructuralist trauma theory, Rivers's theory of trauma presents an alternate frame through which to view Barker's realism. Rivers provides a model of trauma that reclaims realism as therapeutic and an inevitable part of the healing process. Instead of dismissing realism as a form that makes trauma easily consumed due to its penchant for narrative closure that is often interpreted as catharsis, realism for Barker is necessary in both the psychoanalytic treatment of shell shock and narrative representing such treatment. (Steffens 2014: 47)

Rivers heals his patients by turning their dreams into a realist narrative. By acting as a symbolic agent according recognition to the characters, the reader is akin to the analyst. Rita Felski parallels reader recognition and political acknowledgement to promote a new understanding of the affects of reading:

> When political theorists talk about recognition, however, they mean something else: not knowledge, but acknowledgement. Here the claim for recognition is a claim for acceptance, dignity, and inclusion in public life. Its force is ethical rather than epistemic, a call for justice rather than a claim to truth. (2008: 29–30)

In her analysis of reader responses to *Small Island*, collected from a variety of book clubs and designed to 'disentangle real readers from ideal readers' (Lang 2009: 126), Anouk Lang identified characterization and reader identification as paramount in accounting for the success of Levy's book. The very complexity of reader identification is related to 'the tension between attracting and repelling reader sympathies'

(Lang 2009: 134). This tension is engineered by characterization which is sympathetic towards the characters despite the fact, or maybe because, it outlines their very human limitations. This served Levy's purpose of consciousness raising about race issues by engaging the readers in a far from easy recognition process which makes room for differences: 'The complexity of characters on both sides of the race divide prevents readers from settling into an easy identification with either. What the responses to *Small Island* suggest is that readers were simultaneously drawn to the central characters and yet kept from full identification with them by their less enticing characteristics, thus preserving the integrity of their difference' (Lang 2009: 133).

Those limitations were skilfully woven into the first-person viewpoints she adopted to often comically dramatize the misunderstandings born of a cultural clash between the idealized metropolis and the blanked-out colony, prompting the readers to interrogate their own perspective: 'By revealing the often severe limitations of its characters' – both British and Caribbean – understandings of each other's nations and indeed each other, the text can be seen as having prompted these readers to interrogate their own perceptions however briefly' (Lang 2009: 130). This complex characterization corresponds to what David James has termed Levy's 'collaborative realism': 'This participatory experience is equivalent to, indeed a component of, Levy's collaborative realism: she invites readers to negotiate complex gradations of pity and distance, compassion and critique, amusement and discomfiture – all of which are components informing, rather than detracting from, the way we admire how scenes are visually and tactilely realized' (2014: 62).

Additionally, that the readers are let in on the family secret of the progenitor of Queenie's mixed-race child given to the care of Hortense gives them a responsibility in according recognition to the characters' common story. Queenie and Hortense never discover that they both know the father of the child, Michael Roberts, Hortense's surrogate brother and her secret sweetheart. By letting the readers in onto the secret of miscegenation, Levy calls for their acknowledgement of the British–Caribbean collective history, a call which is echoed in Churchill's quote that concludes the novel. The words of Churchill – 'Never in the field of human conflict has so much been owed by so many to so few' – take on new meaning in the novel's context of the nation's rebuilding: 'Through this concluding dedication, Levy captures the sense of owing. [. . .] She not only honors brave RAF servicemen (among whom were Caribbean men), but within the context of her novel, she more broadly refers to the black "pioneers" who came to London from 1948 onwards and contributed to the making of contemporary Britain' (Duboin 2011: 31).

By electing minor characters prone to abjection or self-abjection, Barker, Levy and Tremain do not call on the readers' self-recognition but on their susceptibility to issues of social inequity. Abjection counters narcissism in the realist text by calling on empathy – 'suffering with' – that transcends class, gender or race. Reconciling the usually opposite notions of shock and recognition in her phenomenological approach to reading, Rita Fleski highlights how the everyday and the avant-garde need not necessarily be opposed but are rather more enmeshed than poststructuralist theory would have it: 'the everyday phrase "the shock of recognition" [. . .] underscor[es] that glimpsing aspects of oneself in a literary text is far from straightforward experience' (2008: 133). Reconnecting with the initial democratic impulse of the classic realist novel, contemporary women novelists use the everyday life of common people to shock their readers into awareness of social wrongs, class divisions, gender and racial divides. The readers are invited to actively contribute to the characters' reconstruction thus encouraging a sense of individual liability in building a communal life.

4

Realist characterization and the feminist politics of location

Situated knowledges

Reading implies adopting the perspective of the characters. It means immersing oneself in the consciousness of another, especially with novels written in the first-person or using third-person internal focalization. To borrow from Donna Haraway, reading is 'an instrument of vision' that 'mediate[s] standpoints' (Haraway 1988: 586). Realist characterization calling on the readers' affect favours critical positioning once the readers recognize their partiality in engaging empathetically or antipathetically with characters. The characters' 'partial perspective' (Haraway 1988) mirrors the readers' own and encourages an examination of the convergence or divergence of views. While in 1970, Barthes declared that 'what is obsolescent in today's novel is not the novelistic, it is the character; what can no longer be written is the Proper Name' (Barthes 1974: 95) because it sustained the realistic illusion of a person, contemporary women novelists today use characterization to problematize situated knowledges.

Situated knowledges derive from the feminist standpoint theory that accords epistemic privilege to minority groups. Realist characterization fleshes out points of view by embodying ideas in characters. In line with the classic realist tradition, realist characterization often focuses on marginal personalities struggling to fit in the world. The larger the cast of characters the more polyphonic the world views included in a novel. However, while recognizing the epistemic privilege of the subjugated, situated knowledges aim at reconstructing objectivity. Haraway says it is not enough to simply belong to a minority. What is needed is a critical stance that produces knowledge within the limits of their partial perspective and that further endeavours to connect with differing viewpoints.

Even though Haraway likens what she calls the 'god trick of seeing everything from nowhere' (Haraway 1988: 581) of traditional science to omniscience, it is my contention that contemporary omniscience precisely embodies the feminist objectivity that assumes its partiality and tries nevertheless to present 'heterogeneous accounts of the world' (Haraway 1991: 199). By bringing together and offering unprecedented access to different consciousnesses, the realist omniscient narrator produces human knowledge.

Every writer has a motto which relates to writing as knowledge production. Rose Tremain unusually taught her students at UEA to 'write about what [they] don't know'. She is interested in adopting unfamiliar perspectives and favours marginal characters for their unconventional outlooks on life:

> It has to do with a feeling that I have that people who are not valued or are marginalized or are experiencing difficulties vis-à-vis mainstream life in some way are likely to have a more unique and original perspective on life. And I believe that's what I'm after, this voice from the wings, 'dans les coulisses,' emphatically not on the main stage but from this kind of . . . tangent. (Menegaldo 1998: 107)

The short story 'My Love Affair with James I' is made up of the writing exercise of an ageing actor attending a creative writing class. It sums up Tremain's own view of writing as deriving knowledge from experience:

> For instance, do I, through my recent experience, actually know more about the following: James I, Georges Villiers, Will Nichols [a fellow actor], the psyche of actors, the price of success, seventeenth-century English civilisation, twentieth-century Greek civilisation [where the film was shot], love, infatuation, envy, childhood, Welsh miners and so on? I'm not sure. But all these are vital ingredients in the knowing of something I can only fully understand by writing about it. (Tremain 1999b: 173)

In 'Blocked', Zadie Smith facetiously adopts a first-person narrator that can be either herself as a writer experiencing a writing block or God who is undergoing a depression, thus playing with the notion of the omniscient god trick. She contrasts her early career novels peopled with crowds of character:

> When you're young you try to prove you can do it all, anything – you throw everything and the kitchen sink in there! You're profligate! You've got this sense of unlimited potential. You think you contain multitudes, and in my experience you kind of *do*, at that age, because you're still sufficiently flexible to contain multitudes, you haven't drawn lines around your shit yet and there is still something ineffable about you, something that can make space for whatever is *not* you. (Smith 2019a: 202)

with her own partial perspective today: 'But I know how *I* feel. That's what you get left with, in the end: a very precise and intricate sense of how you yourself feel. Which is not nothing' (Smith 2019a: 202). This has led her to relinquish control: 'control is an illusion' (Smith 2019a: 205). The guiding principle of Smith's writing is that of changing her mind and of producing knowledge based on feeling. Her overall feeling of unbelonging is what defines her writer self, as she said in an interview: 'I think of myself as somebody not at home, I suppose. Not at home anywhere, not at home ever. But I think of that as a definition of a writer: somebody not at home, not comfortable in themselves in their supposed lives, in their nation, in their bodies, in everything' (Dwyer 2019).

White Teeth and *On Beauty* were multivocal novels because of their large cast of characters. *NW* experimented with writing to translate the inner cacophony of Lea and Natalie. *Swing Time* focuses on a first-person narrator who is invaded by the world's discord. This multivocality relates to the author's own personal experience as a mixed-race woman and as a low-born who ascended to international fame. In 'Speaking in Tongues', Smith explains about her 'double voice' (Smith 2011: 133) and cites the experiences of 'the tragically split': immigrants, transsexuals, mulattos (Smith 2011: 136). Her non-fiction keeps articulating this fracture by regularly opposing twin figures: Barthes and Nabokov, McCarthy and O'Neil, Hepburn and Garbo. *Swing Time* gives the split a bodily turn by calling forth dancing: not just being split but doing splits. A month ahead of the publication of the novel, Smith dedicated an article in *The Guardian* to the great dancing figures she once again arranged in opposite pairs: Gene Kelly and Fred Astaire, Michael Jackson and Prince, Nureyev and Baryshnikov.

The voice experiments in her novelistic characterization echo her writer's double voice. *White Teeth* and *On Beauty* experimented with large polyphonic casts to problematize the individual's relationship to groups and communities through a variety of family situations. Individual crisis within the family epitomizes issues of citizenship within society. *White Teeth* focuses on first- and second-generation immigrants through the mingled stories of the Iqbals, the Joneses and the Chalfens. Dialogues display the characters' divergent points of view as well as emphasize 'the heteroglossic function of the novel form' (Bentley 2007: 496) while the third-person omniscient narrator constructing the storylines bridges the gaps opened up by family feuds and colonial legacies. This narrator, that Paul Dawson has called 'pyrotechnic',

> is typically humorous or satirical, and relies less on moral introspection or historical research than on a flourishing and expansive narrative voice, a garrulous conversational tone, to

assert control over the events being narrated. Omniscient authority is a product of the narrative level which determines a narrator's relationship to the characters, and of the manner in which this relationship is articulated to the readers. (Dawson 2009: 153)

The comic mode which connects readers, characters and the narrator has been identified by Nick Bentley as that of Horatian satire: 'the dominant mode of the novel is comedy, operating mainly through a form of Horatian satire picking out unavoidable foibles, hypocrisies and moral expediencies of the main characters' (Bentley 2007: 497). Horatian satire aims to redress people's follies and foolishness through ridicule. Joyously celebrating hybridity and miscegenation by using the tradition of English satire, the narrator 're-imagines a multicultural interpretive community that corresponds to the kind of plural society presented in the text' (Bentley 2007: 498). The final scene reuniting the characters together at the FutureMouse© scientific presentation is indeed built up by the narrator as a pyrotechnic finale in which fanatics of all sorts – religious fundamentalists, activists, scientists – are thwarted and a baby will be born whose father could be either one of the twins, Magid or Millat. The unborn child whose undecidable paternity 'symbolizes an escape from the ideological weight of colonial genealogy' (Bentley 2007: 500) echoes the genetically modified mouse. FutureMouse© indeed gestures towards Haraway's OncoMouse™ which she uses in *Modest_Witness@* to figure how technoscience might offer an escape from blood and genetic legacies to produce 'a diffracted sort of family romance' (Haraway 1997: 78).

As illustrated by the ending of *White Teeth*, Smith favours the 'middle line' of Forster 'when defending his liberal humanism against fundamentalists from the right and left' (Smith 2011: 14). She pays homage to Forster's *Howard's End* in her third novel, thus modifying the traditionally confrontational relationship between hypertext and hypotext in postcolonial writing. Smith follows in the footsteps of Forster in her interrogation of the sociocultural issue of aesthetics.

With *On Beauty*, the narrator's voice turned ethical to pursue the question of kinship both inside and outside of the family unit:

> What draws Smith to Forster and, in particular, to the 1910 classic is her precursor's relational imagination [...] setting forth the strong emphasis Forster places on disinterested ties, friendships and affective bonds, humans affiliations, and generally on the other's nurturing proximity to the self no matter how far apart the two may be by location, ethnoracial background, or political allegiance. (Moraru 2011: 133)

Characterization and plot in *On Beauty* are determined by sets of binary oppositions articulated around the aesthetic issue:

> Underlying these individual and often interacting strands of plot is a deeper narrative structure made up of competing terms along a series of aesthetic binaries, which gives meaning to each element of the plot beyond its immediate, causal significance within the narrative. Binary pairs include white/black, thin/fat, Mozart/hip-hop, Rembrandt/Haitian art, and beautiful/ugly. This underlying structure is made intelligible [...] in the thematic connections between the characters' individual stories. (Anjaria 2008: 38)

The characters embody political and social notions that their domestic life dramatizes and puts to the test. Howard Belsey's conceptualization of anti-aesthetics is proven wrong when he favours a thin white woman for his mistress while his Black wife Kiki struggles with menopausal overweight. Weaving together knowledge and feeling, the text defeats the pretensions of the disconnected intellectuals Howard and Monty in favour of Carlene's and Kiki's embodied perception of art. The departure from Forster's plot, that the inheritance is a painting rather than a house and that it actually passes to Kiki, tackles head-on the notion of a bond formed by mutual recognition beyond differences and by aesthetic valuation: 'clearly, in Smith's novel, the painting takes up the role of the house in *Howards End*, signifying what the two female characters have in common—their intuitive understanding of beautiful things and human emotion—and forming a spiritual tie between them' (Urano 2012).

Smith continued to explore friendship ties in *NW* and *Swing Time* whose protagonists are pairs of female childhood friends. In *NW*, the rift between Leah and Natalie is materialized by their social environment and their relationship to motherhood. Leah still lives on the council estate where they grew up and works as a social worker. She lies to her husband about stopping birth control as she does not want children. Keisha, who has changed her name to Natalie, has become a successful barrister and has married an investment banker. She raises her two children in a Victorian house in an expensive neighbourhood of London but also engages in extramarital affairs online. In *NW*, Smith experiments with a variety of narrative techniques that contrasts internal and external views so that the characters are as much self-defined as they are defined by their intersubjective relationships. The experience of the body is strongly contrasted with the characters' social identity. Natalie uses sex to escape the pressure of the social expectations she endeavours to meet while Lea feels pressured into lying about her lack of desire for children. Smith contrasts acknowledgement and self-knowledge: the body characterizes what escapes sociality.

On the diegetic level, the characters experience solitude, which Smith's experimental writing transcribes, while on the extra-diegetic level, the characters' experience can only be apprehended in relation to one another. Mutual characterization, like dialogues and descriptions, means that realism enables connections while modernist writing emphasizes solipsism. Thus while Smith situates subjectivity in her mimetic experimental writing that reflects the characters' stream of consciousness, she also opts for feminist objectivity as defined by Haraway in her realist account of intersubjective crossings: 'here is the promise of objectivity: a scientific knower seeks the subject position, not of identity, but of objectivity, that is partial connection' (Haraway 1988: 586). By connecting characters whose self-identity is confused, Smith the writer produces her own critical positioning and empowers the reader to connect the dots.

Swing Time was Smith's first experiment with a first-person narrator. The novel continues to build on the inspiration of Elaine Scarry's text. Smith furthered Elaine Scarry's notion of the 'unselfing' experience of art which means that pleasure for the spectator derives from being in an adjacent rather than an egocentric position. The fact that the unnamed first-person narrator is adjacent to her own life, being a personal assistant, a 'shadow' in other people's light' (Smith 2017: 4), mirrors the reading experience as a temporary eclipse of the self to penetrate someone else's consciousness but also the writer's own experiment with inhabiting another's mind.

While many critics were harsh with Smith's choice of a first-person narrator they felt was 'dull' (Boyne 2016) and 'unsympathetic' (Bass 2016), it was Dayna Tortorici's contention that 'she has transposed the instructive, contagious voice of her essays into *Swing Time*' (Tortorici 2016). This writer's voice she is often reproached with is the one that transforms her characters' identity strivings into thinking. As Donna Haraway explained, 'identity, including self-identity, does not produce science' and 'subjugation [i.e. the standpoints of the subjugated] is no grounds for an ontology' (Haraway 1988: 534). Similarly, Smith claims that 'identity is a pain in the arse' considering that 'total knowledge of humans' is impossible and that 'everyone is changing all the time' (Armitstead 2019b). Thus her split writer self engages in a conversation with her readers through a variety of literary experimentations and incarnations:

> The split and contradictory self is the one who can interrogate positionings and be accountable, the one who can construct and join rational conversations, and fantastic imaginings that change history. Splitting, not being, is the privilege image for feminist

epistemologies of scientific knowledge. [. . .] The knowing self is partial in all its guises, never finished, whole, simply there and original; it is always constructed and stitched together imperfectly, and therefore able to join with another. (Haraway 1988: 534)

Smith's novels exemplify Haraway's situated knowledges by fictionalizing the split that inspires her writing into characters that struggle to connect. Haraway's 'optics' are translated into the literary notion of perspective which materializes through voice experiments. It is the voice of the writer that connects partially the experiences of the characters through mutual characterization: a character, even a first-person character, never stands alone but comes to life through her interrelations with other characters. Similarly, Smith's novel-thinking emerges in the interrelation with her readers. The reader does not stand alone either, as Barthes would have it, with the text having an independent life of its own, but is conceived of by Smith as a partner to the writer. When Barthes deprived the text of its author, he persisted with a vision of the god trick by disembodying author and reader alike. Smith does not let go of the involvement of the writer in her own text: the text is embodied in the writer and mediates with the reader, thus enabling a connection.

Byatt has also changed her mind over time. In her pursuit of figuring the 'embodied mind', she has, like Smith, lately turned to first-person narrations. Her venture into first-person narratives started with *The Biographer's Tale* published in 2000. In the novel, a student in literature drops his classes to go on a quest for things. In 2003, Sue Sorensen periodized the work of Byatt and reproached her late 1990s work with a lack of humanity in characterization: 'They [the characters in *A Whistling Woman* and *The Biographer's Tale*] never come to life, smothered in their author's ideas about them' (Sorensen 2003/04: 186). Sorensen is right in underlining the overwhelming cerebrality of *The Biographer's Tale* which precisely aimed at disentangling its first-person narrator from the dogmas of poststructuralism and deconstructionism that would have him live in a world of text: 'I began this piece of writing with the moment when I decided to stop being a post-structuralist literary critic' (Byatt 2001a: 214). Writing in 2019, with the hindsight of Byatt's recently published work, it is my contention however that *The Biographer's Tale* was a stepping stone in Byatt's pursuit of embodied writing. The writing project outlined at the end of the novel by Phineas heralds Byatt's own later praxis: 'I could mix warnings with hints, descriptions with explanations, science with little floating flashes of literature' (Byatt 2001a: 257). The sentence provides the blueprint of Byatt's latest novel *Ragnarok*.

Byatt's struggle with *The Biographer's Tale* corresponds to her struggle with writing situated knowledges. For the first time, she used a first-person narrator. However she initially chose to impersonate the fictional Phineas because of her aversion to autobiography:

> I have admitted I am writing a story, a story which in a haphazard (aleatory) way has become a first-person story, and, from being a story of a search told in the first person, has become, I have to recognize – a first-person story proper, an autobiography. I detest autobiography. Slippery, unreliable, and worse, imprecise. (I am trying to avoid the problem of the decay of belief in the idea of objectivity by slipstreaming towards the safer, ideologically unloaded idea of precision. I don't think this tactic quite works.) (Byatt 2001a: 250)

The text reflects Byatt's own conundrum and interrogations. *The Biographer's Tale* was thus a step in managing the kind of objectivity that would mix the 'embodied mind' of the writer with her precise word craft derived from learning. Again, Phineas's words highlight Byatt's own line of questioning with regard to the writer's body:

> I now wonder [. . .] whether *all* writing has a tendency to flow like a river towards the writer's body and the writer's own experience?

I began with what I still consider a healthy desire to *eschew the personal* (the tangential, the coincidental). Yet I am now possessed by a burning desire to describe making love to Fulla Biefield. (Byatt 2001a: 214–15)

While *The Biographer's Tale* adopted the postmodernist convention of metafiction, which accounts for the reader's feeling of a disembodied character, it is my contention that Byatt started to come up with answers to Phineas's questions with the auctorbiographic story 'Arachne' published that same year in 2000.

As mentioned earlier in Chapter 2, the term 'auctorbiography' was coined by Byatt's French translator, Jean-Louis Chevalier, in an interview to describe how such stories as 'Arachne' 'tell things about how [Byatt's] mind, or [Byatt's] sensitivity, or [Byatt's] sensibility, [...] works' (Chevalier 1999: 19).

The story weaves together autobiographic anecdotes about the author's creative inspiration, art ekphrases, a literary retelling of Ovid's tale, a web of literary references on spiders and scientific information on real spiders. It thus combines the author's readings with her writing, the description of things with their knowledge production, imagination with science, thus inextricably connecting the author's personal tangled web of analogical correspondences with the larger history of art painting, entomological science and literature. It is more ekphrastic than it is metafictional thus combining the personal with the descriptive in an efficient tactic which gestures towards Haraway's feminist objectivity by providing 'a reinvented coyote discourse obligated to its enabling sources in many kinds of heterogeneous accounts of the world' (Haraway 1991: 199).

Byatt adopted a similar tactic in her latest novel from 2011, *Ragnarok*. The writer split the story of the Gods of Asgard into a realist narrative of her Second World War childhood reminiscences told in the third person and articulated around the reading of the book adapted from Wagner by M. W. McDowal, an ekphrastic retelling of the northern myth, and a final chapter written in the first-person that elucidates the creative process of the book and which is accompanied by a complete bibliography. The novel references the author's own readings as the crucible of her creative imagination, mapping out the bisections between personal embodied experience and knowledge accretion, actual history and myth-making, thus demonstrating how

> The most straightforward readings of any text are also situated arguments about fields of meanings and fields of power. Any reading is also a guide to possible maps of consciousness, coalition, and action. Perhaps these points are especially true when fiction appears to offer the problematic truths of personal autobiography, collective history, and/or cautionary allegory. (Haraway 1991: 114)

While in 2003, Sue Sorensen estimated that the turn in Byatt's work to observing her own thought processes was detrimental to her novels' characterization – 'once a penetrating writer about the life of the mind, she now writes more restrictively about the life of *her* mind' (Sorensen 2003/04: 189) – it is my contention that it was pivotal in Byatt's later experimental auctorbiographic writing and helped her devise an answer to the body–mind quandary. Her latest piece of writing, published on her eightieth birthday in 2016, *Peacock and Vine*, thus combines the travelogue, the ekphrasis, the personal essay or auctorbiography, human and object biographies.

It provides an illustration of critical situated knowledge as it exposes 'the stakes in location, embodiment, and partial perspective' (Haraway 1988: 584) that are woven together in the author's creative imagination. The starting point of the essay is Byatt's own partial connection between the two polymathic figures of William Morris and Mariano Fortuny. Critics have been harsh with the author's partial perspective criticizing its 'tangential links' (Murray 2016). However, through the enmeshment of art and craft in the two men's lives, Byatt draws her own artistic self-portrait as a craftswoman,

Arachne again, twining together the dresses of Fortuny that inspired Proust's metaphor of the writer as a couturier, and the materiality of Morris's printed words at Kelmscott.

This personal connection was occasioned by a trip to Venice when Byatt could not help but picture English green meadows in her mind while her eyes were 'drunk on aquamarine light' (Byatt 2016: 3). The colour vision that characterizes Byatt's creative imagination prompted her to mediate between England and Italy through Morris and Fortuny. Byatt does not forget that she is a woman: the book begins with an exploration of the artists' marital lives and the adjacent position of Jane, the woman object in pre-raphaelite paintings, and Henriette, the shadow assistant of her husband. Byatt's own photographic portrait is taken at the Museo Fortuny below the portraits of Henriette. Byatt acknowledges her husband Peter and his patience with 'the usual habits of writers', underlining how domesticity and the quotidian anchor her creativity. She is taking a stand as a woman artist. She is also drawing attention to herself as an embodied artist through the uncommon inclusion of portrait photos while she hates her photographic self: 'I have come to hate being photographed, and to hate the existing photographs that reappear in my life from time to time' (Byatt 1998). Because it is an auctorbiography and because her portrait dialogues with the other portraits in the book, in particular those of Henriette, so Byatt allowed the inclusion of the photo. In addition, the last photograph of the book is a close-up on her hands writing in the notebook she always carries along with the scotch tape she also constantly fingers and which an interviewer described as a sort of rosary, highlighting the way Byatt 'thinks with her fingers' (see Burri 2012).

Contemporary women writers dramatize 'the stakes in location, embodiment, and partial perspective' in realist narratives that cross geographic borders and that toe the demarcation between genders by experimenting with point of views. Interestingly enough, Rachel from Sarah Hall's *The Wolf Border* (2015) and the anonymous first-person narrator of Zadie Smith's *Swing Time* (2016) share similar traits that call into question self-knowledge and perception in relation to female embodiment. Both characters are successful professional women travelling around the world with no strings attached. They are examples of the Western ideal of the 'economic man' that Mary Mellor describes as 'young, fit, ambitious, mobile, and unencumbered by obligations' (Mellor 2000: 113). At the beginning of the novel, Rachel is working in Idaho on an Indian reservation as a result of a successful European career and has happily left her family problems behind back in England. The narrator of *Swing Time* has similarly detached herself from her overbearing mother, to the point that she learns only very late that her mother has cancer, and from her childhood friend Tracey who has psychiatric issues, in order to travel the world with the rich and the famous. The dancer figure epitomizes, in the narrator's view, this unanchored male sense of identity: 'But to me a dancer was a man from nowhere, without parents or siblings, without a nation or people, without obligations of any kind, and this was exactly the quality I loved' (Smith 2017: 24).

Maternity is what comes as a life-turning experience for both characters. Rachel initially goes back to England to have an abortion, which is prohibited in Idaho. She accepts a job offer from Lord Pennington and decides to keep the baby. Eventually she will take responsibility for her addict brother, forge a bond with her veterinary boyfriend and his daughter, and care for her own child. The narrator in *Swing Time* will rebel against her pop star boss' shady adoption of an African child. She will also rebel against her mother's suggestion that she should revoke Tracey's parental rights for her own good. The adjacent experience of surrogacy in its legal dimension – the illegal adoption of the African child and the legal action her mother suggests she takes against her friend – prompts the narrator to question her own lifestyle and to finally emancipate herself from her own mother's injunctions. The novel thus closes with the narrator visiting Tracey: 'I almost turned back, like someone who has woken abruptly from a sleepwalk, except for an idea, new to me, that there might be something else I could offer, something simpler, more honest, between my mother's idea of salvation and nothing at all' (Smith 2017: 453).

The legal issue is also of paramount importance in Hall's work. She systematically calls on legal administration issues, in particular territorial law, as a background to her characters' struggle with their minority status. It is through this weaving together of regional planning and subjective identity that Hall manages to put in perspective situated knowledge by contrasting geographic anchorage, state and regional governance, and the actual embodied experiences of her characters.

Her first novel, *Haweswater*, was inspired by an Act of Parliament from 1919 that authorized the Manchester Corporation to build a reservoir to provide water for the urban conurbations of northwest England. By mentioning the former name of Westmorland, the epilogue of the novel alludes to the Local Government Act of 1972, which reorganized local administration into metropolitan and nonmetropolitan counties and districts. The love story between Janet, the Cumbrian farmer, and Jack, the Manchester overseer, incarnates and dramatizes the administrative divide. Janet's tragic fate – she commits suicide trying to blow the reservoir after Jack has died and she has had his baby – is set against the local population's powerlessness in the face of state administration. Prior to her suicide, the very status of Janet as an unmarried pregnant woman is juxtaposed with the past administrations of labour and poverty: 'Her mother will not have her sent to the workhouse for unmarried women in Penrith' (Hall 2016a: 208). Her fragile mental state when she self-mutilates after Jack's death also allows for allusions to the mental health laws of the time and the medical discourse on female disorders, which her mother also saves her from: 'There will be no asylum, no madhouse sanatorium for Janet Lightburn.' (208). *The Carhullan Army* similarly parallels women's rights and land administration by speculating on a process of Civil Reorganization which has curtailed local powers in favour of the dictatorial Authority and has 'written off' (Hall 2017a: 20) some citizens from the census who then become Unofficials, like Sister herself, the nameless narrator.

Hall's latest published novel *The Wolf Border* parallels territorial administration and species management by referring to the Land Reform of Scotland and the Zoo Licensing Act or the French Louveterie through which Charlemagne ordered the destruction of wolves. Her speculative fiction about rewilding Britain ends with the wolves' escape to Scotland, a land favourable to sustainable development. She also draws a parallel between regional and family planning by having Rachel relocate from a pro-life American state to England to get an abortion. While in Idaho, Rachel lives on an Indian reservation and Hall also refers to issues of land sovereignty.

By systematically connecting legal issues regarding women's reproduction rights with spatial planning that enforces a masculine domination over both the social and the natural environment, Hall's fiction calls for an acknowledgement of the 'sex/gender inequality in the construction of human-nature relations' (Mellor 2000: 119). By locating her characters, including her non-human characters, within the moving administrative borders of Cumbria, on the historically contested borderlands with Scotland, by embodying these struggles in their bodies, in particular the pregnant body, by judicially connecting the minority groups subjugated by the laws of the land, Hall's fiction displays an affinity with Haraway's situated knowledges as 'siting (sighting) boundaries':

> Boundaries are drawn by mapping practices; 'objects' do not pre-exist as such. Objects are boundary projects. But boundaries shift from within; boundaries are very tricky. What boundaries provisionally contain remains generative, productive of meanings and bodies. (Haraway 1988: 595)

In Sarah Hall's novels, the women's bodies, in particular the bodies marked by the agricultural activity, refract the landscape. The embodied female experience echoes environmental interconnections. In *Haweswater*, Janet's body is attuned to the region's seasonal cycles:

> She has been pressed between two vast mountain ranges [. . .] each year she is re-forged. She accepts the weather and the ability of the rain to overwhelm all else. [. . .] Her body chemistry alters as the terrain decomposes, turns, begins again. [. . .] She has given herself over to this saturated strip of Westmorland. (Hall 2016a: 112)

In *The Carhullan Army*, the agrarian women resistants have also been re-forged by farming in the Cumbrian uplands: 'they did not look like girls, middle aged and older women. They seemed to be sexless, whittled back to muscle by toil and base nourishment, creatures who bore no sense of category, no dress code other than the one they chose. [. . .] strong, resilient' (Hall 2017a: 118–19). The women characters in Hall's novels embody the notion of 'weathering' developed by Astrida Neimanis and Rachel Loewen Walker as 'the intra-active process of a mutual becoming' (Neimanis 2014: 560): they are both attuned to the weather, changed by it and bearing with it; just as they modify the landscape through agriculture, they are similarly modified by their relationship to the land.

Cumbria, in Hall's novels, is a cultural landscape layered with 'spacetimemattering' (Barad 2007: 234): it is broached through its geology, its human history, its natural and agricultural features, its human and non-human populations, its weather patterns. Historical strata overlap in *Haweswater* when the construction workers of the dam of 1936 are compared to the border reivers (Hall 2016a: 163) and the army that has come to blow up the village of Mardale are likened to the Roman legions (219). The skeletal buildings of the destroyed village itself are anachronistically paralleled with concentration camps, thus showing that 'the past and the future are enfolded participants in matter's iterative becoming' (Barad 2007: 234). Similarly the futuristic speculations of *The Carhullan Army* are based on reimagining the past: the final battle of the resistant women at Rith – altered Penrith – takes place at the medieval defensive castle that Hall relocates on Beacon Hill. Cumbria in Hall's novels is a transcorporeal entity that is both spatialized and temporalized. Thus, situated localized knowledge echoes a larger current change of paradigm in envisaging bodies as measured through human time and space within the environment's larger scales of geological mutations and meteorological phenomena.

The people inhabiting the Cumbrian terrain are similarly layered. Hall varies the adopted perspectives of men and women and describes the changes wrought by experience. In *Haweswater*, Jack, the urban overseer from Manchester, at first attacks the landscape through his climbing activity. His masculinist view of nature as something to be dominated is likened to the cases of woman abuse previously described in the text. The landscape is depicted in bodily terms: Jack climbs

> as if aiming at volatile levels of an imaginary human body with a knife, a fist. He spins between crevaces, punching shadows in the solar plexus, as if he wants to outmaneuver and overwhelm the nerve system of the mountain as he would an enemy. It is a strange skill, this blind murder of landscape. (Hall 2016a: 128)

The scene is reminiscent of that of domestic abuse Jack witnesses from the window of his hotel room in Penrith when a man is 'kicking blood from his wife's stomach' (91) and a young woman is gang raped by three men (92). His own grip on a prostitute's face performing fellatio anticipates his hold on the rock face of the fells: 'a hand over the mouth of one, forcing indentations into her cheeks, bringing her to his groin' (92). Falling in love with Janet, he will later try to atone for his early conquering attitude towards her native region by bringing back the trophy eagle he initially bought for himself to her eyrie. He dies in the attempt.

In *The Carhullan Army*, the gap between the present world of the reader and the future world of the novel in which a despotic Authority regulates birth control through the mandatory fitting of coils is materialized by the altered relationship between the narrator, Sister, and her husband Andrew. Sister experiences marital rape when Andrew, excited by the gel left from the coil fitting operation, penetrates her while she consents only out of habit: 'I wanted to ask him to stop [. . .] but neither one of us had ever said no to the other' (Hall 2017a: 29). The forced intrusion is manifested by the absence of quotation marks when the text records the words of Andrew: 'Sex was one of the few remaining pleasures, he said; it was nice to feel me without any barriers' (31). This experience is what triggers Sister's enrolment in the Carhullan army. In *The Wolf Border*, the absence of quotation marks in the novel's dialogues exposes the artificiality of borders: the omission of the conventional marker mirrors the indifference of the wolves as to the arbitrary perimeters humans decide to draw on their maps.

In Smith's case, the use or non-use of inverted commas is related to social issues. In *Swing Time*, the use of inverted commas is related to the narrator's adjacent position. It transcribes the way that she experiences herself as a 'shadow in other people's light' (Smith 2017: 4). In the novel's prologue, in which this 'truth [is] being revealed' (4) to her, she quotes from her conversation with a doorman to illustrate her sense of exile from England: 'I had been out of England long enough that many simple colloquial British phrases now sounded exotic to me' (2). As a personal assistant, she has become used to recording and interpreting the language of Judy, the manager of her celebrity boss. When she suggests readings to Judy: 'she would give one of four possible judgments. "Zippy" – which was good; "Important" – which was very good; "Controversial" – which could be either good or bad, you never knew; or "Lidderary", which was pronounced with a sigh and an eye roll and was very bad' (133).

The narrator is deferring to other people's assertions just as she used to with her fanatic college boyfriend raving against the "'establishment'" (288) and "'Jewish Hollywood'" (290), himself being "'conscious'" (287) while she is reproached with living only in "'simulacra'" (291). She gives herself over for a time to Rakim because she has failed to fit with the narrative of "'the first in our line to go'" (287) as her own mother has just completed a degree and criticizes her daughter's university.

The narrator's mother is a strong feminist who engages in a political career after the completion of her degree. The narrator feels that her mother delivers to her the same lines she gives to the journalists, which is materialized by the quotation marks. About her mother's partner and, as the narrator thinks of her, her foil, Miriam, her mother repeats the same sentence: 'the journalist from the *Willesden and Brent Times* got exactly the same line I'd been given: "Miriam makes me happy"' (151). Pop star Aimée's words to the press are also quoted with the punctuation marks signalling the clichéd emptiness of her words: 'I heard her tell the *Rolling Stone* reporter how important it was to stay "in the real world, among the people"' (204).

In addition to the delivery of their expected cues, characters also dress the part. Throughout the narrator's childhood, her mother thus sports linen trousers, a "'Breton'" T-shirt and espadrilles to signify her difference from the rest of the neighbourhood and her ambition to "'get out of here'" (10). The boyfriend Rakim – whose very name is an alias borrowed from a rap singer – 'wore skinny dreadlocks to his shoulders, Converse All Stars in all weather, little round Lennon glasses' (288). The characters are depicted as walking semiotics dressed in their belief systems. The lines they deliver, bracketed by quotation marks, are similar to the familiar tunes of popular songs that regularly surface in the text. The novel dramatizes the song and dance of the post-Saussurean world. It is significant in that light that the narrator, who remains undecided as to her own beliefs, has no name. Smith reinterprets Barthes's pronouncement by embodying a character struggling with inauthenticity. It is not the referential illusion that is being challenged. Rather, the novel explores what it means to be a person in a world which has defeated the reality effect.

Contemporary texts dramatize the difficulty of connecting rationally and imaginatively with our differences and contradictions. Hence the repeated warnings about the dangers of fantasy when it encourages solipsistic self-delusion. Sarah Hall's short story 'Evie' engineers a shock in the reader contrived through a violent clash of the male character's perspective with reality. The story of Evie's sudden change of sexual behaviour is told from her husband's point of view. Although he is worried at first by his wife's unusual comportment, he is quickly carried away by his own appetite for sexual experiments. The story depicts orgiastic scenes of pornographic sex until Evie has a massive seizure. The final revelation that she was the victim of a brain dysfunction that lifted her inhibitions shocks the reader into realizing, like the husband does, that the supposedly consensual sex was in fact abusive. Like Barker and Carter, Hall uses pornography to problematize sexual difference. The delusion does not depend on the referent but on the character's point of view: it is not reality which is illusory but the character who is delusional and willingly suspends disbelief to indulge in his sexual fantasies. The reader is forced to confront the moral issue of sexual abuse by experiencing complicity with the perpetrator through the adopted perspective.

Similarly in Byatt's short story 'The Pink Ribbon', the reader experiences the powerlessness of a husband faced with his wife's Alzheimer. The husband's disgust and anger at his wife's helpless state and child-like mind is transcribed through his colour optics. He wickedly decorates her hair with a pink ribbon while she always hated pink because of its 'babyish' aspect (Byatt 2004a: 219). He buys her the green Teletubbie Dipsy because 'it's a slightly bilious green and the name's appropriate' (205). He himself renames her 'mad Mado'

(228) and he stabs the doll with hairpins as he would a voodoo doll, which echoes the text's reference to zombies. The red doll Po, to his mind, is even more cruel: "'Po is even nastier,' he said defensively. "Potties it means. Pot-bellies.'" (219). In contrast with the husband's perception of reality coloured by his own rage, Byatt introduces a fantastic element to support the helpless character of Madeleine. She is a Fetch, a doppelganger self of the diseased woman, who intercedes in her favour with her husband, implicitly asking for euthanasia. With this figure, the references turn literary: her name is Dido, whose figure in Virgil emblematizes loyalty to her husband and suicide; the Teletubbie Po turns into a reference to the Po river in Virgil which is one of the rivers of Hades; the actual name of the woman, Madeleine, refers to Proust's *Search of Lost Time* that problematizes memory.

The story, published in the 2003 collection *Little Black Book of Stories*, was Byatt's response to John Bailey's 1999 memoir about his wife, Iris Murdoch's descent into Alzheimer, in which he recorded how he would put her in front of the television to watch the Teletubbies. In Byatt's estimation, what Bailey did, writing about his wife's condition, was 'wicked' and 'unforgivable' (Leith 2009). Introducing the Fetch in her own narrative to contradict the husband's perspective was Byatt's way of honouring Murdoch's literary imagination. It tackles the moral issues of euthanasia, marital intimacy and spousal abuse through cross perspectives that bisect sexual difference.

The story also repeats Byatt's constant preoccupation with the body–mind dilemma. From the onset of her famous Quartet novels, she has looked to representing the conflict between embodied experiences and the life of the mind as traditionally conceived of as disincarnate. The female characters in Byatt's novels struggle with the biological demands of motherhood as opposed to their intellectual ambitions. A Cambridge graduate, the oldest sibling in the *Quartet*, Stephanie, eventually marries a pastor and forsakes her career to raise her two children. She is killed in a freak accident with a refrigerator in *Still Life*. Would-be writer Frederica manages to escape an abusive marriage and to juggle a successful TV career with single motherhood in *A Whistling Woman*. The sheer number of characters in Byatt's novels echoes the multi-focal view her narrative technique promotes.

By multiplying the perspectives from embodied experiences, Byatt avoids the trap of 'the god trick of seeing everything from nowhere' (Haraway 1988: 581) that is usually associated with omniscience. Thus a sentence from *Still Life* exemplifies Byatt's work with mediated refractions: 'A girl crosses the courtyard in a yellow dress and can be seen, optically, amorously, medically, sociologically' (Byatt 1995a: 335). The signifier 'girl' usually denotes nubile seduction like the yellow dress she is wearing. The reader expects the white male gaze from nowhere to take over the description of the girl in the yellow dress. However the addition of various adverbs transforms the omniscient gaze into a multiplicity of contextual interpretative possibilities. The unidentified third-person pretence to objectivity from the beginning of the sentence is shattered by the adverbial connotations that refract the variety of possible mediating optics on the girl.

Byatt's highly visual writing accords with the optics favoured by Haraway. Van Gogh's paintings are the inspiration behind *Still Life*. Byatt meant to connect the visual impact of Van Gogh's realist still lifes with the novelistic world of her characters' bodily experiences: 'Byatt meant *Still Life* to be a "plain novel about birth, marriage and death" and about "biology described from very close up, in language," she said in a 1996 radio interview with Eleanor Watchel' (Sorensen 2003/04: 65). The connection she endeavours to draw between words and things, between thinking and feeling, is what she calls 'self-conscious realism' that 'leaves space for thinking minds as well as feeling bodies' (Byatt 1993: xv). She locates this consciousness in the ordering eye: 'even the most innocent eye does not simply receive light: it acts and orders' (Byatt 1995a: 131). Byatt's partial perspective, her feminist objectivity, is thus located in the tension between the chaotic biological life and the artistic ordering gesture that inclines towards perfect stasis. This tension is more particularly connected to the female conflict between mind and body represented in her work by the stone women figures: 'The frozen, stony women became my images of choosing the perfection of the work, rejecting [. . .] the imposed biological cycle, blood, kiss, roses, birth, death, and the hungry generations' (Byatt 2001b: 164).

By experimenting with the narrative voices of realism in the first and the third person, by incarnating the individual struggle within the collective social life and the embedded environment, by pitting different perspectives against one another in characters that come to be mutually self-defined, realist women writers manage to give form to feminist objectivity and accountability. Their work with the points of view of embodied consciousnesses situates knowledge by drawing partial connections through omniscient narration and mutual characterization.

5

Realist descriptions
Re-inscribing democracy

The fact that realism incarnates ideas, identity struggles and moral dilemmas in the bodies of its characters serves to highlight the function of its characteristic descriptions. The everyday objects that populate the characters' world testify to the texture of reality that they perceive as embodied consciousnesses embedded in their environment. I would like to draw a parallel between Jacques Rancière's distribution of the sensible and Stacy Alaimo's transcorporeality to mark the contemporary specificity of realist descriptions. It is Rancière's contention that classic realist depictions, far from being superfluous, were in fact a way to redistribute the sensible by according the same amount of attention to daily objects, animals or the weather, as to the human characters. For Rancière, who takes the example of the barometer in Flaubert's story 'Un Coeur simple' in reference to Barthes, the insignificance of the daily items mirrors the dramatization of the minor lives that realist writers brought to light (2014: 23). The texture of reality is that of the type of life that they live. This is the reason why Rancière equates literature with politics in that it gestures towards a democratic redistribution:

> There are two contrasting structurations of the common world: one that knows only of *bios* (from transmission through bloodlines to the regulation of population flows); and one that empowers

artifices of equality, that is, forms enacted by political subjects to refigure the common of a 'given world'. Such subjects do not affirm another type of life but configure a different world-in-common. (2010: 93)

While Rancière still adopts an anthropocentric view which posits the object as a reflection of the human lived experience, the posthuman critical turn challenges the perception of the world-in-common by advocating a planetary democracy where the human no longer is the centre of the world, by according *zoe* the same place as *bios*:

I have argued that *zoe*-centered egalitarianism expresses the simultaneously materialist and vitalist force of life itself, *zoe* as the generative power that flows across all species. The new transversal alliance across species and among posthuman subjects opens up unexpected possibilities for the recomposition of communities, for the very idea of humanity and for ethical forms of belonging. (Braidotti 2013: 103)

Stacy Alaimo has offered transcorporeality as a concept to figure 'the posthuman being' as 'entangled with the very stuff of the world' (2014: 16). Realist description today reconfigures characters and objects as phenomena tangling the social with the material. As Alaimo says about Barad's 'intra-actions': 'Tracing intra-actions and other modes of entanglement between substances and systems enables political critique and the development of ethical and political modes that do not separate the human from the material world' (2014: 15). This neo-materialist change of paradigm has its roots in the feminist social movement with its emphasis on the body and in feminist epistemology and science philosophy which challenged the Cartesian tradition of a transcendental knowing subject.

The return to the material experience of the body in material feminisms 'via their insistence that the human body is, simultaneously, a political, ontological, and epistemological site' (Alaimo 2014: 16) means that they re-appropriate second-wave feminist theories such as Julia Kristeva's abjection or Luce Irigaray's fluid mechanics. It is the case, for instance, with Elizabeth Grosz who uses Kristeva to connect women's lived experience of their bodies with what she calls their 'modes of seepage', or how the cultural imaginary of women's bodies as leaking fluids influences women's empirical perception of their own flesh and sex:

> My hypothesis is that women's corporeality is inscribed as a mode of seepage. My claim is not that women have been somehow desolidified but the more limited one which sees that women, insofar as they are human, have the same degree of solidity, occupy the same genus, as men, yet insofar as they are women, they are represented and live themselves as seepage, liquidity. (1994: 203)

Pat Barker's detailed attention to fluids in her descriptive writing is meant to make the reader aware of women's lived experience of this internalized cultural mode. It relates to the abject dimension of her writing insofar as she parallels the disgusted feelings aroused by those fluids with the crude materiality of the vocabulary she uses. She quite literally figures the impropriety of the female sex by using realist description as a shocker to make plain to the reader the way that women live their corporeality. Like her naturalist forebears, she uses slang, not however to document scientifically the sociology of her characters, but to provide the reader with a direct experience of the violence of seeing one's body as offensive. To Barker, words are like phlegm: 'The words felt solid and sticky in her mouth like phlegm' (1999: 42).

Barker's descriptions function as contamination. In *Union Street*, the impact of the rape on Kelly is materialized as a skin irritation that translates the porosity of barriers that no longer operate: 'her skin seemed to have flared up into an intense and irritable life of its own' (Barker 1999: 36). The collapse of the boundaries between her intimacy and the outside world means that she now sees everything around her as contaminated with a disgusting viscosity:

> On the surface she felt . . . a revulsion from surfaces. The dishcloth had left slimy smears all over the table. The slipperiness disgusted her. Everything disgusted her. [. . .] Most of all she hated the remembered texture of his jacket, the moist, lard-whiteness of his skin. (36)

The traumatic experience changes the very texture of reality. The use of adjectives is of paramount importance as they signal the alteration of Kelly's perception. The nouns which identify the commonplace objects that populate Kelly's world are modified by the tainted adjectives that repeat the sensations experienced during the rape. The predicates mirror Kelly's predicament. The 'slimy smears' on the table echo the earlier 'mess of blood and slime on her thighs' (34). The focus on the jacket's texture and on the sensation and colour of the rapist's skin, 'moist, lard-whiteness', transcribes the heightened sensory perception of a traumatized consciousness. Although, in Kelly's story, the environment is largely urban and man-made, the term 'viscosity' cannot help but bring to mind Nancy Tuana's concept of 'viscous porosity' in her interactionist approach to hurricane Katrina:

> There is a viscous porosity of flesh – my flesh and the flesh of the world. This porosity is a hinge through which we are of and in the world. I refer to it as viscous, for there are membranes that effect these interactions. These membranes are of various types – skin and flesh, prejudgements and symbolic imaginaries, habits and embodiments. They serve as the mediators of interactions. (2008: 199–200)

Barker gives a new dimension to the everyday and the mundane by displaying the texture of reality as unbounded by trauma. Far from being the superfluous details that Barthes condemned in realist descriptions, the adjectives express the full resonance between the individual consciousness and the stuff of the world. The breaking down of Kelly's intimate, material barrier, her virginal membrane, entails the dissolution of the solidity of the world. Thus, while Mary Douglas – whose anthropological work on impurity influenced both Kristeva and Grosz – made a difference between different types of fluids, postulating that tears did not inspire revulsion as opposed to seminal and digestive fluids, the viscous porosity felt by Kelly determines all liquids as goo. Her traumatized perception contaminates the rapist's tears which she perceives as senseless: 'and now moisture of some kind was oozing out of the corners of his eyes' (37). His face which 'was beginning to split, to crack, to disintegrate from within, like an egg when the time for hatching has come' (37) anticipates Kelly's revulsion at her own mother's breakdown: 'she felt, rather, distaste for this woman whose hard exterior had cracked to reveal an inner corruption. Her mother had been the one solid feature in the landscape of her mind' (60). The dissolution of the frontiers between inside and outside, adult and child, liquid and solid, is further materialized when Kelly goes roaming at night in the derelict neighbourhood that is home to the marginalized or when she breaks into her school and into a bourgeois house so that trauma manifests the intangible frontiers that structure society by dramatizing their collapse.

John Brannigan has called the omniscient narrator that weaves together the female experiences of rape, abortion, prostitution, poverty, pregnancy, birth, death, sickness, an 'omnipresent narrator' that is on an equal footing with the characters through shared language:

> *Union Street* is, in this sense, an experiment in closing the gap between the authoritative voice of the omniscient narrator and the recorded language of the characters. The 'community' of the novel is only possible through the distance of the extradiegetic narration, but Barker's narrator is able to be omnipresent without straying beyond the knowledge and idiom of her community. (2005a: 30)

Thus, even though the novel describes the harsh reality of its female characters in a disintegrating neighbourhood, the omnipresent narrator constructs a community by going from one chapter to the next like Iris goes from house to house on Union Street. The book itself is the world-in-common.

Similarly, Bernardine Evaristo's latest Booker-prize winning *Girl, Woman, Other* entitles its chapters with the twelve characters' first names and uses their many experiences to 'span from a teenager to someone in their 90s, and see their trajectory from birth, though not linear' (Sethi 2019). The plan for the book was to make visible the experiences of Black women: 'I wanted to put presence into absence. I was very frustrated that black British women weren't visible in literature. I whittled it down to 12 characters' (Sethi 2019). Though not from the same neighbourhood, most of the characters get together at a theatre performance with the metaphor of the world as a stage reinforcing the visibility issue. The language used is that of her characters as is most evident with teenage characters like Yazz or immigrant characters like Bummi. Evaristo's narrator could similarly be described as omnipresent insofar as its voice is the one that sketches a communality based on equal literary treatment between diverse ages, sexes, races. Although the plot is not linear – but neither is Barker's – the text does have some components of realism, especially the verisimilitude of the characters' psychology coupled with the third-person narrator who offers the reader an insight into their everyday lives and minds with the use of free indirect speech. Evaristo is experimenting within the conventions of realist writing. This latest novel is her fourth prose novel and it is Sara Upstone's contention that Evaristo's turn to prose fiction with *Soul Tourists* 'represents a further movement towards realist convention' (2017: 31). Like Barker in such novels as *Another World*, Evaristo used the supernatural in *Soul Tourists* to picture the hauntings of history within 'a contextually harshly realist' text (Upstone 2017: 31).

Descriptions in *Girl, Woman, Other* connect the political issue of visibility with the material issue of the body and the cultural topic of fashion dress. A characteristic feature is the upbeat rhythm of the many adjectives that reflect the dynamism of political activism as an energizing liberation from the dress codes of proper attire. Amma is a representative of the counter-culture movement of the 1980s, modelled on Evaristo's own experience. The adjectives mirror the energy of hybridizing cultures, languages and styles:

> she wants people to bring their curiosity to her plays, doesn't give a damn what they wear, has her own *sod-you* style, anyway, which has evolved, it's true, away from the clichéd denim dungarees, Che Guevara beret, PLO scarf and ever-present badge of two interlocked female symbols (talk about wearing your heart on your sleeve, girl). (2020: 3)

The adjectives themselves are all phenomena transposed from another initial grammatical category: slang – '*sod-you*' – foreign nouns – 'clichéd' 'denim' – proper name – 'Che Guevara' – abbreviation – 'PLO'. Evaristo others linguistic propriety just as her activist character wilfully others herself in a bid for freedom. This descriptive style redistributes the semiotics of advertising in a humorous way as the character's free indirect speech depicts her former outfit with irony while paying homage to their then enthusiasm for undressing the part. The unabashed spirit of fashion eccentric Amma is contrasted in the next paragraph with her daughter's plea for normativity. Yazz 'recently described her style as "a mad old woman look, Mum", pleads with her to shop in Marks & Spencer like normal mothers' (2020: 3), while her millennial generation also uses fashion as a statement like her friend who wears a sequined hijab.

The ballet shoes in Zadie Smith's latest novel *Swing Time* similarly serve to embody the generational gap between activist mothers and millennial daughters while also mediating class, family, body and memory issues. The anonymous narrator meets her childhood best friend Tracey at a dancing class. While their similar skin tone makes them befriend one another, the ballet shoes materialize their different family situations and contrasting maternal bond. The narrator resents her feminist mother who is able to seek advice as to where to find the cheapest shoes. By contrast, Tracey's mother spares no expense to dress Tracey in the latest fashionable outfits: 'she was her own mother's most striking accessory. The family look, though not to my mother's taste, I found captivating: logos, tin bangles and hoops, diamanté everything, expensive trainers of the kind my mother refused to recognize as a reality in the world' (2017: 10). As a result, the narrator, who lives with both her parents and is not on benefits, is the only one in her class not to have the pink satin shoes emblematic of the standard ballet outfit:

> Almost everybody had the pink satin shoes, not the pale pink, piggy leather I was stuck with, and some – girls whom I knew to be on benefits, or fatherless, or both – had the shoes with long satin ribbons, criss-crossing round their ankles. Tracey, who was standing next to me, with her left foot in her mother's hand, had both – the deep pink satin and the criss-cross – and also a full tutu. (14)

The accumulated adjectives depicting in detail the texture and colour of the shoes transcribe the narrator's envy and frustration with her own pair. Later on, Tracey proves to be a gifted dancer with 'rhythm in individual ligaments, probably in individual cells' (26) while the narrator is impeded by flat feet. The never-to-be dancing career is further aggravated by the revelation of the narrator's East Ender father's other family. The narrator meets her white half-sister who also happens to have had a scholarship at the Royal Ballet school. And so the remembered shoes encapsulate the whole childhood world of parental monitoring and the parallel bubble of adult missteps and betrayals, the unexpected attachments of friendship and its vexations, the utter devotion to celebrity idols. The shoes are the very fabric of memory. They are the material mediators between different time planes – childhood and adulthood, the materialist era of Thatcherite Britain and the narrator's present – between social spaces – the upper-class Royal Ballet, the dancing class in the high rises – between sexed and raced bodies – the history of Black dancing, the musicals' partner dances. They also exemplify Smith's experiment with the first person of putting herself in someone else's shoes.

A materialist approach to the sartorial politics of Black feminism outlines the entanglement of the social, the textual and the material. The visibility issue is tackled through the spacetimemattering of clothing one's body which is mirrored in the way the plentiful elaborate modifiers primp the sentence to evoke the many clad bodies of different eras and social spaces. In *Soul Tourists*, while cruising through Europe, Stanley also travels in time when he interacts with the manifestations of a place's history which materialize censured Black and mulatto figures as the untimely matter of the archival European past. What Sarah Adams calls Evaristo's 'hip-hop signature' queers the temporal by 'meshing timeframes, juggling spoken and narrative registers, fusing the glaringly incompatible, and, here, flipping between free-style verse, prose and dramatic dialogue' (Adams 2005).

The realist sentence characterized by its attention to adjectival details serves a purpose of giving reality a specific texture. Descriptive writing gives its grain to the fabric of reality and renders the sensory experience of the characters as they move through the social world with bodies that are at one and the same time organic and cultural, spatial and temporal.

Pat Barker's offensive writing materializes the internalized perception of women as seeping taboo fluids while it offers moments of reprieve with 'its recurring use of the natural world as a metaphor of grace' (Ward). The tree unites the first and last chapter, the beginning and the end, the teenage girl Kelly Brown and the elderly Alice Bell. For Kelly, who has been ostracized by her experience, the tree full of singing birds 'like the sound of women talking and brushing their hair at once' (1999: 65) stands for home, the collective she wishes to rejoin. Alice with her bird-like appearance – 'the old woman's hands were like bird's claws', 'the throat that in its nakedness was as vulnerable as a bird's' (67) – helps Kelly on her way back home by arousing compassion in the girl for her tears. For Alice, the singing tree helps her come to terms with her impending death as she will then become other. Already her body is turning into vegetable matter with her legs like 'root vegetable, a turnip or a parsnip' (227) and her hands resembling dead leaves: 'brown, discoloured, the flesh wasting away between raised veins' (240). Holding hands with young Kelly, she embraces the vision of cyclical life as materialized by 'the withered and unwithering tree' (241).

By contrast, Smith and Evaristo's relish with the adjectival appendages of the sentence expresses their delight at creating reality's textures as sites of resistance. By making visible the experiences of Black or mixed-race characters as delectable, they counter the long history of odious racism. Evaristo's repeated use of food descriptions transcribes this gourmet-like approach to luscious texturizing. There is material pleasure in the savour of food, the fabric and colour of clothes, the body's movements in dancing, the mnemonic melodies of pop music, that the carefully crafted sentences transcribe. For Smith, this pleasure is directly connected to the everyday and to observation that characterizes her writing life. In an essay for the *New York Review of Books* entitled 'Joy', she evokes food as a daily pleasure and a relief from the anxiety of writing, especially eating pineapple popsicles, and parallels it to the pleasure of observing 'other people's faces' (Smith 2013). She then proceeds to give detailed depictions of people met on the street that she rushes back home to share with her husband. She defines writers as 'professional gawkers' (Smith 2013).

Observing people's features gives rise to imagining the fabric of their reality. Again, writer and reader are very much alike in that reading is also close to gawking at someone else's lives and thoughts. The realist description invites the reader to share the reality of other people in exhilarating and upsetting ways: to experience the harshness and the humour of women from the northern working class, the frustrations and the ambitions of a mixed-race millennial, the joys and the fears of an elderly gay Caribbean in Evaristo's *Mr Loverman*.

For Byatt too, there is relish in the choice of adjectives and observation is the key to descriptive writing. Like Barker, Smith or Evaristo, she reinterprets the female experiences of the everyday as a creative crucible. Her colour vision explains her singular ekphrastic art. What fascinates Byatt about colours in words is their grammatical indeterminacy, hovering between nouns and adjectives:

> I think the names of colors are at the edge between where language fails and where it's at its most powerful. One of the things I noticed when I was working a lot on van Gogh in *Still Life* was how he doesn't decline his color adjectives. It is as though all the colors remained things. So if you're talking about *quelque chose blanche* he just leaves it as *blanc*. Apparently you're allowed to do this because it isn't quite clear whether they are nouns or adjectives. That in itself is very beautiful. (2011b)

Van Gogh's colours as things recalls Byatt's intent to capture the 'thinginess' of things. This, in turn, calls to mind Plato's discussion of forms in the *Republic*, with craftsmen and artists in search of the bedness of beds, one of which is ekphrasis. Charles Riley has noted how, in relation to Van Gogh's, 'Byatt takes the step up from marking a grammatical point to construing a "Platonic pattern of eternal forms". The passwords to this ideal realm are ostensibly the color terms' (1995: 268–9).

Byatt has devoted a humorous realist short story to the question of representation in its relation to artifice. In *The Matisse Stories*, which situates itself in the ekphrastic tradition with its reproductions of Matisse drawings as story headings, 'Medusa's Ankles' narrates on a comic mode the epic crisis of a middle-aged woman at her hairdresser's. The decoration of the salon triggers the crisis. At first elected by Susannah for its comforting boudoir-like aspect expanding on the reproduction of Matisse's Rosy Nude, it is then turned by its owner into a harsh hall of mirrors in cold dark colours mixed with an ominous red.

The ekphrastic depiction of the salon's interior mirrors the protagonist's state of mind: the girlish pink and creamy tones console her for the loss of her once luscious hair. She trusts the hairdresser Lucian to 'render natural-looking, that was, young, what was indeed natural, the death of the cells' (1994a: 7). Susannah emblematizes 'the internalization of our culture's denial of and distaste for aging, which is understood in terms of decline, not in terms of growth and change' (Woodward 1999: xiii) and the further process of social exclusion through undesirability for old women more particularly.

Susannah's crisis happens at the moment when she has reached the height of her professional career which requires her to appear on TV: 'the cameras search jowl and eye-pocket, expose brush-stroke and cracks in shadow and gloss. So interesting are their revelations that words, mere words, go for nothing' (1994a: 20). The social fate of ageing women to appear unnatural is further dramatized by Susannah's memories of her own mother's hairdressing sessions: 'Her mother had gone draggled under the chipped dome of the hairdryer bristling with metal rollers, bobby-pins and pipe-cleaners. And had come out under a rigidly bouncy "set", like a mountain of wax fruit, that made her seem artificial and embarrassing, drawing attention somehow to the unnatural whiteness of her false teeth' (6).

Instead of a critique of the referential illusion as nature's copy, Byatt's text offers a criticism of the social interpretation of the natural process of female ageing as aberrant and abhorrent. In her last novel,

Wise Children, Angela Carter expanded on that very same theme with the seventy-five-year-old narrator Dora explaining: '[it is] every woman's tragedy [. . .] that, after a certain age, she looks like a female impersonator' (1992: 192). Both writers use the comic to raise the awareness of the readers as to their prejudices about female ageing. Byatt's use of the rose colour is highly ironical and fuels the comic process. Quoting Wallace Stevens, she once wrote about 'the comic colour of the rose' (Byatt 2010). The comforting pink colour migrates from the allaying modifier that used to bathe Susannah's reflection in a 'deceptive rosy haze' (1994a: 16) to a verb of action characterizing her transformation into a destructive Medusa, wrecking the salon, petrifying its customers: 'Rage rose in her' (23). This shift of word class from the adjective to the verb is emblematic of Byatt's overall metonymic poetics. Instead of one word replacing another as in a metaphor, the metonymic process makes visible those linguistic transfers by emphasizing a sense of contiguity. This is Roman Jakobson's theory on 'The Metaphoric and Metonymic Poles' who further determined metonymy to characterize literary realism: 'Following the path of contiguous relationships, the realistic author metonymically digresses from the plot to the atmosphere and from the characters to the setting in space and time' (2003: 43).

This metonymic process is pivotal in the implementation of the story's comic which relies on contiguous displacements. Thus, Medusa's frightful hair is comically displaced in the ordinary context of a hair salon defeating the Freudian interpretation of her consolatory penis-like curls. Similarly, the story's title displaces the question of Medusa's gaze, traditionally representative of the male gaze in psychoanalytical readings of the myth, onto her ankles. The text elicits this choice of title when Lucian explains he has left his wife for a younger woman because 'she's let herself go altogether. She's let her ankles get fat, they swell over her shoes, it disgusts me' (21). It is male vanity that is being condemned along with the social judgement on female ageing. Susannah's very name, in a story laden with iconographic references, evokes the pictorial tradition of representing the biblical tale of Susannah and the Elders. The painting's very absence in the text, only referred to through the protagonist's name and contrasted with the actual presence of Matisse's *La Chevelure* as the story's heading, underlines the invisibility of old women in European paintings except as harbingers of madness, greed or death. The biblical story itself is that of a woman invaded in her privacy and condemned for her refusal of male advances. Byatt thus offers her own interpretation of the myth as an intermedial tale on female midlife crisis.

Hair is an interesting material–semiotic node striding the divide between nature and culture, between interpretations of what's natural-looking or artificial-looking, as Kobena Mercer outlines: 'nobody's hair is ever just natural but is always shaped or reshaped by social convention and symbolic intervention' (1987: 38). Hair turns political in Black women's writing as the history of Black hairstyles tangles materiality with politics, sociology, fashion and the everyday. The activist mothers in Evaristo's *Girl, Woman, Other* and Smith's *Swing Time* sport an Afro, the politicized hairstyle made popular by the Black Power movement and the Black is Beautiful movement that encouraged Black people to own their difference as a badge of honour. In Evaristo's novel, the noun of the hairstyle is turned into an adjective, 'her afro'd compatriots' (2020: 41) which signals the activist prospect of devising a new collective identification. By contrast, Shirley, Amma's conservative childhood friend, straightens her hair: 'her mother put her under the hot iron comb at the age of twelve and she hasn't seen or felt her real hair since' (2020: 427).

The Afro that leaves the original texture of the hair intact was thus deemed more natural-looking while straightening meant conforming to the white standards of beauty. In her first novel from 1994, *Every Light in the House Burning*, Andrea Levy devotes a chapter to Angela's first straightening session at the hairdresser. The place is emblematic of the Black people's condition in England in the 1960s: there is no salon in the neighbourhood where Angela lives so that with her mother and sisters they have to cross London, and for the first time Angela is surrounded with Black people, 'I had never been in the company of so many black people before' (2016: 166). On the radio, the news discuss Enoch Powell's 1968 'rivers of blood' speech. Although Angela has to undergo the chemical burning feeling on her scalp and a three-hour long drying session that also feels like burning, she is happy with the result that allows her to blend in: 'After all the pain, here was my reward. Straight hair. Manageable hair. Not my hair, but hair like my friends – not different' (172).

In Smith's novel, starting in 1982, the narrator's mother's hairstyle, a very short Afro, combined with her plain dressing style and absence of make-up amount to a political statement: 'in this way her financial circumstances, her politics and her aesthetics were all perfectly – conveniently – matched' (2017: 10). The materiality of hair testifies to the political and cultural history of the Black diaspora in Britain.

Like the Afro, dreadlocks 'sought to "liberate" the materiality of black hair from the burdens bequeathed by racist ideology' (Mercer 1987: 40). They were however quickly appropriated by white subcultures. In Evaristo's *Mr Loverman* the teenage daughter Donna falls in love in the summer of 1977 with a white heir to an estate who rebels against his inheritance by adopting the Rasta look and calls himself Shumba. Barrington assumes Shumba will ultimately conform to his class expectations by becoming an investment banker and going hunting (2013: 136). He is proven wrong at the end of the novel when his grand-son, who has become friends with Hugo's son, tells him that Hugo/Shumba sold his father's estate to engage in philanthropist work (301). The polymorphism of texturized hair reflects the manifold cross-cultural interactions between Africa, the Caribbean and England, between mainstream culture and counter-culture, innovation and imitation, liberation and confinement. The final emancipation of Carmel from her marriage to gay Barrington is signalled by her change of hair once she comes back from Antigua:

> As for her hair. *What-a thing.*
> When I first met Carmel, her hair was the product of a hot-iron comb; as she got older she dyed it; and it started to thin prematurely from all she put it through, she bewigged herself.
> Now look at her: *au naturel*, and, I have to say, it looks bloody lovely. (2013: 275)

On her trip back to the Caribbean, Carmel comes across the former wife of her husband's lover, Odette, who has decided to dispense entirely with her hair by shaving 'not because she got alopecia but because she'd decided to go from high-maintenance to no-maintenance *on principle*' (285). Odette berates the Black hair industry, adding the economic dimension to the political, cultural and gender facets of hair.

The adjectives that describe the textures of hair are of paramount significance in tracing the distributions of the sensible. They help to interrogate the notions of the natural and the real. The nouns of the hairstyles in their sheer variety challenge the racist identification and classification of 'nigger hair': the cornrows, the conk, the Afro, the locks, the braids, the curls, the weaves. They redesign the perception of reality as inventive routine anchored in the material praxis of hairstyling at the same time as they rewrite Black history as both material and cultural resistance: 'black peoples of the African diaspora have developed distinct, if not unique, patterns of style across a range of practices from music, speech, dance, dress and even cookery, which are politically intelligible as creative responses to the experience of oppression and dispossession' (Mercer 1987: 34). Hair is not just a metaphor of the entanglements depicted by Karen Barad, they are the tangible threads that allow one to 'sight boundaries' and thus move them across time and space to design new commonalities.

The prologue of Andrea Levy's *Small Island* thus criticizes imperial scientific racism that segregated Black people as inferior based on physical features. On her visit to the 1924 British Empire Exhibition, the child Queenie's description of a Black man relays the racist stereotypes commonly circulated by colonial iconography like the gollywog figure from children's books:

> But then suddenly there was a man. An African man. A black man who looked like he had been carved from melting chocolate [...] A monkey man sweating a smell of mothballs. Blacker than when you smudge your face with a sooty cork. The droplets of sweat on his forehead glistened and shone like jewels. His lips were brown, not pink like they should be, and they bulged with air like bicycle tyres. His hair was wooly as a black shorn sheep. His nose, squashed flat, had two nostrils big as train tunnels. (2009: 6)

The adjectives focus on the two signs of difference that racist ideology selected to biologize otherness and attribute essentializing meanings and values to racial others: skin colour and hair texture. The comparisons used by Queenie underline the imperial economic dominion she has just wandered through – the sheep from New Zealand, the chocolate from Grenada – as well as the industrial revolution – the tyres, the train, the mines. Thus Levy weaves together the parallel commodification of the merchandises and of the people from the British colonies. The scene outlines the physical – both biological and geographical – boundaries that were drawn by the colonial power to order a value system:

> In discourses of 'scientific racism' in the seventeenth and eighteenth centuries, which developed in Europe alongside the slave trade, variations in pigmentation, skull and bone formation and hair texture among the species of 'man' were seized upon as signs to be identified, named, classified and ordered into a hierarchy of human worth. The ordering of differences constructed a 'regime of truth' that could validate the Enlightenment assumption of European 'superiority' and African 'inferiority'. In this process, racial differences – like the new scientific taxonomies of plants, animals and minerals – were named in Latin. (Mercer 1987: 35)

The aim of posthuman and new material feminism is to question scientific taxonomies, or to phrase it along the lines of Barad's theory, to understand the agential cuts made in the phenomena in order to break down the barrier between observer and observed. Realistic writing, with its focus on descriptive writing, is particularly suited to explore the compass of predicates and redistribute adjectival attributes, as Byatt wrote in *Possession*: 'vocabularies are crossing circles and loops. We are defined by the lines we choose to cross or be confined by' (1991: 431). Realistic women's writing is attentive to the sensory experiences of texturizing the world with words, and challenges the lexical assignments of values to empirical incarnation.

The tension in Byatt's writing between a taxonomic enterprise of naming things and the unravelling of that same process in dizzying metonymies that fracture the word's unity to open up unexpected analogies relates to the female conundrum between body and mind, the mess of the everyday and the perfection of art. Just as Smith's writing is split between the readerly and the writerly, so Byatt's is divided between stasis and metamorphosis. Time and again, her short stories oppose twin artist figures emblematic of her quest. In 'Art Work', she opposes the Black cleaning woman Mrs Brown who turns daily objects like people's discarded clothes into fantastic knit creatures and her white boss Robin, a 'neo-realist before neo-realism' (1994a: 52) obsessed with 'his vision of colour' (1994a: 56). In 'Christ in the House of Mary and Martha', inspired both by the biblical story and Velazquez's painting, Byatt confronts the angry young cook of the picture to the quiet master painter. Both stories are articulated around binaries: male/female, master/servant, white/Black, old/young, action/contemplation. However the narrators of those stories are not the protagonists, they are positioned at one remove from the dilemma represented in the twin figures: 'Art Work' is told by Robin's wife, Debbie, and 'Christ in the House of Mary and Martha' by the older servant, Concepción. This adjacent position mirrors the story's

Realist Descriptions

ultimate focus on ekphrasis: the depiction of fabrics, textures and objects is what matters echoing the lesson of Velazquez: 'the divide is not between the servants and the served, between the leisured and the workers, but between those who are *interested* in the world and its multiplicity of forms and forces, and those who merely subsist, worrying or yawning' (1999: 226). The world's textures allow one to exit ego-bound solipsism and reach out to the real world out there in a reciprocal 'contact' as Byatt said in an interview:

> I suppose what I mean by 'work' is not the same as the Protestant work ethic, because it isn't about self-denial and self-betterment. It is a space for a passion that isn't personal and isn't necessarily affection for other people. I've always been interested in why Velazquez' best painting was actually the surfaces, the things – the eggs in *Christ in the House of Martha and Mary*. Similarly, the expression on the face of that very angry servant girl in *Christ in the House of Martha and Mary* haunts me, and she haunts me partly because she is in the same picture as this perfectly painted egg – they balance each other. This is where the really difficult, complicated, beautiful things are, this contact between oneself and the world. (Tonkin 1994: 26)

Byatt's latest writing has further implemented a turn towards things which expresses the complex enmeshment of the human and the non-human. In *Little Black Book of Stories*, her latest collection from 2003, the piece entitled 'Raw Material' focuses on the ekphrastic pieces written by Cicely Fox, an elderly participant to a writing class. 'How We Used to Black-Lead Stove' and 'Wash Day' unravel the endless 'intra-actions' of matter in human everyday life that the colour semiotics of black and white nuances paint. The domestic activity of black-leading weaves together the geological origins of coal, its use as a fuel combustor, an analogy with the human digestive combustion of matter, the toxicity of industrial fumes and lead cosmetic paints, human death rites in the form of burial or cremation, the semiotics of advertising with the furnace's trademark 'Phoenix', the fairy-tale imaginary of cinders. All those nuances are evoked in the many different blacks of the glossy coal and the matt coke, the metallic black-lead applied on the 'blackest black' furnace (2004a: 172). The differential colours express something of the 'contingent quiddity' of things (2004a: 168) as standing between the ideal form and the phantom representation. Thus commenting on Edmund de Waal's pottery, Byatt writes about his pots as she would about Mallarmé's rose: 'A glossy black pot makes a light in darkness – a matt black pot absorbs light from the shiny pot and from the lead around it, becoming a kind of memory of a pot' (2014).

The memory imprinted on the iris by the light's reflection is similar to the white ghosts, fluttering and dangling from the pegging line in 'Wash Day'. This piece evokes a world of smells at a time when cleanliness required massive everyday toil and was achieved through uncountable alchemical conversions. The temperature and steam in the wash house 'full of extremes of watery climates' (2003: 182) mean that the prevalent odour was that of the sweat of labouring bodies and of the dirt being cleansed from the clothes. There was the 'evil' smell of bleach (184) and the smell of ironed starch which 'was like a parody of cooking': 'You could smell scorching as you could smell burning cakes' (186). So that 'you had a nose for things not as they should be' (186). The religious subtext of cleanliness and dirt as good and bad complexifies the relationships between natural and chemical odours, the mess of bodily fluids and laundry hygiene. The strange conversion effected by Reckitt's Blue that turns the whites whiter or by the delicate operation of starch that must be properly timed to obtain the correct result can be interpreted in the light of those innumerable entanglements that belie any clear-cut divide between the natural and the cultural. 'Gluey', 'slippery' starch (185–6), the vegetable matter that was used to prevent dirt from penetrating the cloth's fibres, is akin to the viscous porosity described by Nancy

Tuana as 'the dance of agency between human and nonhuman agents' (2008: 198).

Although Cicely's fellow students reproach her story with the absence of 'living human interest' (177) and criticize her adjectives, her pieces inspire in the writing teacher, Jack Smollett, a renewed interest in his students: 'They made him see the world as something to be written. Lola Secrett's pout was an object of delighted study: the right words *would be found* to distinguish it from all other pouts' (189). This complex interaction between oneself and the world is further complicated by the story's ending when Jack finds Cicely's corpse which bears the traces of years of abuse.

The appropriation, by all the authors under study, of the semiotics of advertising allows to measure the modification feminism effected in relation to Marxist materialism. By uncovering the repressed forms of domination buried under commodity fetishism – simply put, that the subordination of others (women, gays, coloured people) and of nature as commodities is the foundation of the Western capitalist ideal – feminism has radically modified the very notions of things and values. New material feminism offers a critique of capitalism along with a novel perspective on justice and accountability based on the upheaval of subject/object relations. Realistic writing as appropriated by women writers is highly significant in that regard as the depicted objects of realism have long been associated with a bourgeois order of *things*, both as the images of commodification (including that of literature) and as the emblems of a value system that perpetuate as natural the regulation of social relations.

Rose Tremain's Neo-Victorian novel, *The Colour*, perfectly captures and transforms the stakes of commodity fetishism with a tea box. The symbol, par excellence, of British colonialism, the tea box serves two different functions for the main couple of protagonists. Joseph Blackstone uses it as a hiding place for his find, the gold nugget, which ultimately turns to shit, as he labours in the crap mines that disfigure the New Zealand landscape and abuses a teenage boy with multiple anal rapes. By contrast the label of entwined herons on the tea box foretells the unexpected prospect of Harriet Blackstone who finds love, for a brief utopian time, with a Chinese vegetable grower who originates from Heron Lake, and will carry and raise his child with the help of their own gold find, thus emancipating herself from her marriage of convenience, a single mother raising a mixed-race child. The same matter is invested with different sign values that give rise to two narrative paths. The tea box may be interpreted as a material–semiotic node that engenders multiple storylines. Material feminism in the line of Donna Haraway and Karen Barad is about recognizing the agential cuts we effect in our entangled relationship with the world in order to take responsibility for how we affect it. The tea box exemplifies the possible stories generated by those cuts. Harriet's storyline is the moral one because she takes responsibility for her love story and the child to be born. Women writers lay claim to the ethics of realism which today coincide with the ethics of vulnerability.

This chapter focused on the epistemological implications of naming the world. The next chapter will further investigate the ontological consequences in writing of this new democracy of things.

6

Posthuman naturalism

The realist novel today takes stock of a changing epistemological paradigm that ultimately modifies the ontological relationships between characters and settings, humans and non-humans, causes and consequences, temporality and spatiality. In literary terms, it modifies the relationships between reader, writer and text, between novels, essays and short fiction, that become much more intimately entangled as varied mediators of an empirical experience of reality. Writers use poetic language to depict the phase transitions between states of matter as exemplary of endless porous mutations. Astrida Neimanis has used water as the substance that best exemplifies the posthuman feminist endeavour to 'undo the idea that bodies are necessarily or only human' (2017: 2). That she lays claim to Merleau Ponty's embodied phenomenology (see Neimanis 2013) signals the primacy of empirical experience in knowledge production. In turn, recharging science with perception entails remapping ontological divides. Thus, considering that the human body is made of two thirds of water, Neimanis looks at how 'as bodies of water we leak and seethe, our borders always vulnerable to rupture and renegotiation' (2017: 2). She has forged the term 'hydrocommons' to designate 'the interbeing of bodies of water' (2009: 161).

The prologue of Sarah Hall's *Haweswater* outlines the hydrocommons between man, land, animal and weather through interspecies analogies that blur the boundaries between kinds and give rise to a watery imaginary that ruptures the ranks of genera and phenomena. Thus the rain pouring on the face of the unidentified man in the prologue – who will turn out to be Janet's father Sam – turns him into straw by blurring skin and hair tones: 'The man's face and his hair melted into each other and both were the colour of red straw. Children could have landed safely in this face from a high jump off a barn rafter' (2016a: xii). The dog that accompanies him is transformed into a seal: 'her slick seal's head slicing the waves' (xi). The thunder and hills are modelled on human biology: 'A cough of distant thunder in the throat of hills to the north-east' (xi). Water is a semiotized body running through the landscape: 'The rise and fall of the water's tensile voice. Its sound was unusual, a continuance of text in a land of broken fluid, of forced rock' (ix).

The combination of *soma* and *sêma* in the natural-cultural body of water is declined throughout the novel in the polymorphous water states. There is the water of the reservoir whose drowning force reverberates with the biblical Flood – especially as the chapter titles of the book read like the biblical annotations of chapter-verse. The icy waters of the upland lakes characterize Isaac, Janet's brother, depicted as a watery creature who will become a professional diver and ultimately drown on purpose in the reservoir, completing the ritual sacrifice of his biblical namesake. Janet herself dies by fire. This holocaust of children – as the text also refers to the death camps – is echoed in the death of Nathaniel, the repository of the valley's story who survived his offspring. This story of extinction, mirrored in the killing of the female golden eagle – a species that Hall anachronistically revives as it only appeared in the region in the 1950s and disappeared in 2015 – is also a story of creation. The book opens with the breaking waters of Ella giving birth to Janet.

The forces of extinction and creation are mirrored in the contrast between the domination of the water resource by state planners and engineers, helped by the army, and the watery bodies of the valley's inhabitants that have appropriated the aqueous terrain. Thus Janet, swimming in a waterfall's basin, appears to Jack as 'a statue of rain' (136). The dichotomy between domination and appropriation has been theorized by Henri Lefebvre in his study on the production of space. Using a water lexicon, one could contrast hydrologic engineering with the hydrocommons of the valley. However, even though the plot of Hall's novel can be summed up with such binaries as rural areas/urban conurbations, male/female, domination/appropriation, extinction/creation, the writing itself strives to paint the inextricable entanglements between diverse forces emblematized by the tragic romance of Jack and Janet.

Hall thus engages in blurring boundaries by using as a setting a border territory characterized by its contested history. She also enlarges the human contests to the more-than-human forces that shaped the landscape. In literary terms, she mixes tropes from the romance and naturalist tropes to develop unexpected cross-phenomena kinships between humans and non-humans. Thus she compares Jack and Janet's love story to a hydraulic force that 'devastates valleys' (254). This romance is born of a 'tellurian pull' (115) between them. The geomechanic force is coloured by the relation implied between earth and its inhabitants. It is Jean-Michel Ganteau's contention that romance 'is notoriously concerned with [. . .] that which escapes realistic investigation' (2003: 237). Hall aggrandizes our phenomenological perception of the world by calling attention on macroscopic time and space. Ganteau further surmises that the androgynous is the emblematic figure of romance that thrives on ambiguity and refuses binaries: 'the androgynous breaks up the traditionally tight, clear-cut, limiting oppositions of the either/or type' (2003: 235). Hall goes further in her posthumanist approach by creating hydrogynous characters. While the passions exposed by romance would traditionally seem to be opposed to the rationale of naturalist inquiry, in Hall's novel there is no such clear-cut demarcation as her ecofeminist writing parallels earth-bound passion and climactic phenomena through a sensorial investigation of the interrelations between human and non-human bodies.

Isaac's knowledge of his sister's suicidal intent is situated in their shared flesh shaped by their native region: 'this is who they are, she and he, people from this carnal realm of water and earth, full of the atoms of this old, dying, re-living place' (231). Hall unexpectedly mixes the fluid water imaginary with the substantial meat imprint, a recurring trope in her work that figures the vulnerable raw flesh of humanity. All of her novels figure minoritarian protagonists struggling against apparatuses of domination from within their own flesh and blood. To use the Deleuzian concepts favoured by such posthumanist thinkers as Rosi Braidotti, Hall draws at one and the same time cartographies of the molar configurations of urban planners, state and regional administration, border control, species management plans, land ownership, and the molecular lines of geological, hydrological, animal becoming of the inhabitants. Those lines of flight design new community groups outside the expected majoritarian divides. Thus Jack escapes the molar patterns of belonging that defined him as a city dweller, a proletarian, a male, to become earth, woman, and bird: 'a truer section of himself had come into being, he felt the infection of it in his blood. That through a metamorphosis in this wild, saturated, palatial land, he was becoming abridged' (148). Empathizing with the female eagle he had ordered killed as a prize, he makes himself vulnerable to death in an ethical attempt to repair his mistake now that he has become minoritarian with being affected by the place he had come to destroy.

The water issue is of particular note in this interrogation of democratic distributions of the sensible. The reservoirs in particular raise issues of minoritarian displaced populations, majoritarian beneficiaries, sanitation and drinking water, of land exploitation, of upset ecosystems, of the microscale of human memories and livelihoods and the macroscale of floods and deforestation. Indian writer Arundhati Roy has famously turned to essay writing for twenty years between the publication of her first novel in 1997 and her second in 2017. She has most notoriously opposed the construction of the Sardar Sarovar dam in Gujarat in her essay entitled 'The Greater Common Good' in which she powerfully questions India as the biggest democracy in the world by pitting the millions of human lives affected by dam building in India, their poverty and lack of access to basic sanitation, against the financial collusions between the state, the dam building contractors and world investors. Rose Tremain's novel *The Road Home*, devoted to the journey of an Eastern European work migrant, Lev, is set against the construction of a dam in his native village of Auror that will rob his mother of the memories of a lifetime. Furthermore the novel draws parallels between various world situations. Ruby, the narrator of Tremain's second novel *Letter to Sister Benedicta* (1978), reappears thirty years later at a retirement home. She tells Lev about her return trip to India where she found out that the convent of her childhood has been converted into a textile manufacture exploiting female labourers. The novel ends with the visit of Lev's Irish friend Christy to Baryn. They go see the dam and the submerged village and Christy compares it to Ireland, paralleling British colonization and the Soviet dominion.

Women writers are working within the framework of realism to develop what Deleuze called a minor literature, working with polylingualism to develop metamorphoses that reterritorialize meaning as 'a distribution of states in the world's fan' (Deleuze and Guattari 1983: 22). Hall uses the accent and pronunciation of her native region in her dialogues along with vernacular vocabulary. Barker uses northern slang. In *Girl, Woman, Other* Evaristo mixes Cockney, pidgin, patois, urban slang, with the Queen's English. In *White Teeth*, Smith mixes Cockney, northern London slang, pidgin, Jamaican patois, Bengali English in what Bénédicte Ledent calls 'a verbal kaleidoscope'. Levy uses Jamaican English, Cockney English and mock standard English. Tremain's novels are often set in foreign countries with characters speaking English inflected by their own native French, Polish, German, most notably in *The Swimming Pool Season*. Allowing for the minoritarian patois of the immigrant, the rural or the lower classes within the majoritarian frame of standard English means allowing for a plurality of potential communities. Hall, more particularly, gestures towards 'radical posthumanism as a position that transposes hybridity, nomadism, diasporas and creolization processes into means of re-grounding claims to subjectivity, connections and community among subjects of the human and the non-human kind' (Braidotti 2013: 50).

Indeed Hall's writing connects together a host of minority cases in the Deleuzian sense: the women labourers, the water and the golden eagle in *Haweswater*; the women labourers and the feral dogs in *The Carhullan Army*; the pregnant woman, the native Indians and the wolves in *The Wolf Border*. This also applies to her short stories that defy traditional majoritarian divides like 'Bees' in *The Beautiful Indifference*. In this story, the second-person woman narrator is an abused woman who leaves the northern family farm for London. Her unemployed status and her raw emotional state mean that she spends much of her time in the small garden of her friend's flat. She wonders about a strange decimation of bees whose cause she cannot identify until she finally discovers that a fox has been killing the bees. The story revolves around border crossings between dichotomous spaces: the city and the countryside, the field and the garden, the human and the animal (see Hansen 2019). The fox is the emblematic intruder that has become adept at transgressing the human urban and suburban demarcations to claim its own habitat unexpectedly. Its omnivorous diet, exemplified in the text by its preying on bees, knows no nutrient bound and earned it its reputation as a scavenger.

The text draws an analogy between the fox and the narrator's exposed, vulnerable insides by way of the colour red. The narrator has fled an abusive marriage that leaves her raw with pain. The narrator feels like a 'loose pink sack of human being' (2012: 71), with 'a freshly gutted body' (172) who has lost a vital part of herself she calls 'that prime red aspect' (71) associated with the survival instinct 'ache, feel hunger, long for' (71), 'that historical red piece that clawed away and is missing somewhere now, that urgeful hybrid creature, carrying flames along its back as it moves' (83). The narrator is in a dissociative state marked by the use of the second person. The missing part of herself reappears at the end of the text in the form of the hunting fox and its fiery imagery, 'as if the creature has been stoked up from the surroundings, its fur like a furnace [...] it shakes its red head furiously' (85). That fearless vitalism, only halfway through domestication, stands for *zoe*, the raw force of life theorized by Braidotti as 'a threatening force, as well as a generative one' (2013: 112).

The anthropomorphic analogy that traces in the fox the most human part of the narrator's self helps to cross the hierarchical border between human and animal, as Jane Bennett advocates: 'a touch of anthropomorphism, then, can catalyse a sensibility that finds a world filled not with ontologically distinct categories of beings (subjects and objects) but with variously composed materialities that form confederations' (2010: 99). The poetic creation of a flaming hybrid creature that seems to have a life of its own and migrates between the woman and the fox defies the ontological divide between them. Similarly, in the rest of the text, the issue of the extinction of species, emblematized by the bees, subtly parallels that of domestic violence, like the female golden eagle in *Haweswater*, while another instance of border crossing – when a one-night stand lover asks to remove his condom which the narrator first refuses and then agrees to – raises the issue of epidemics. The blurred boundaries elicit a new understanding of the nature-culture continuum, the web of complex interactions within environments that escape man-made delimitations.

The confederation of bees-woman-fox as both threatened and threatening also finds an echo in the amalgamation of narrator and reader with the second person. While on the one hand illustrating the character's dissociation, the second person also creates a bond with the reader who cannot but identify with the character. The text thus strides the dichotomous dissociation/association split oxymoronically, or rather schizophrenically, again in the Deleuzian sense: the opposites are conceived of as connected rather than contradictory. The arresting image of the organs fleeing the body – 'something rose up inside your chest. It split you open. It tugged itself through the walls of muscle, slid to the floor and moved off into the crowd' (71) – which then seem to relocate inside the fox, can be likened to Deleuze's 'body without organs' that characterizes the schizophrenic perception as one of pure intensities unbounded by common sense that deterritorializes sociality and allows for new becomings.

Hall's writing reaches towards borderline situations – 'I create survivalist strategies where people are tested, where the urge to keep going comes to the fore' (Garvey 2001) – to strip the social human bare of its common sense vestment:

> What civil lives we lead. So mannered, so controlled. Everything tidy and safe, everything put in its place. How hard we try not to be frightened, not to let the mind and body misbehave, not to come undone. Look at us in our ties and our stockings, taking vitamins and buying prophylactics, arranging mortgages and emptying the bins, ameliorating, ordering. We've almost convinced ourselves.
>
> But underneath, closer than we dare to think, is the reddish nature of humanity, the strong meat of our anatomy. (Hall 2016b: 1)

Sarah Hall devoted another story to the fox figure, her award-winning 'Mrs Fox'. It bears strong similarities with David Garnett's 1922 novella, *Lady into Fox*, recounting from the husband's point of view the transformation of his wife into a fox who will eventually give birth to a litter of cubs. A comparison of the two stories however reveals the change in paradigm effected today by posthumanism. Whereas the lady fox in Garnett's story still retains human habits and behaviour – she insists on dressing up, drinks tea, plays piquet – Hall's fox woman scents the house with her musk, defecates and trashes the place until the husband resigns himself to let her go. In Garnett's, the husband treats her like a pet, calling her Puss, and the cubs Sorel, Kasper, Esther, Angelica and Selwyn, and keeps translating their animal signals into human phrases. By contrast Hall's husband recognizes their otherness and positions himself cautiously as a guest at a distance from the den (2017b: 25). Garnett's story highlights the subjection of both women and animals to patriarchal violence when the husband beats the fox for behaving like a fox, dismembering a rabbit, and when he himself kills the dogs to protect his wife once she has transformed: 'Richard asserts both his patriarchal and anthropocentric superiority – what Derrida would call carnophallogocentrism – through physical violence' (Baker 2019: 83).

Alternatively, Hall's story relates new kinships as the husband experiences a form of surrogate paternity: 'for now, they are hers, and perhaps his, though peripherally' (2017b: 27). It echoes the concluding sentence of the story asserting women's independence: 'how could life mean anything without his unbelonging wife?' (28). Thus whereas in Garnett's, the husband is 'unmanned' by the fox's behaviour he deems monstrous in a woman – tearing the rabbit apart; in Hall's, the husband longs to hear his wife call his name to 'be made un-mad by it' (22). Indeed, in Garnett's story, the metamorphosis is readily accepted and barely described with the story focusing on the domestic life between the husband and the woman fox, whereas Hall's story insists on the wondrous shape-shifting of the body. Sophia as a woman was just as alien to her husband as she is as a fox, the transmogrification simply materializes that difference more radically by bringing to the fore the notion of becoming as a challenge to his set of beliefs: 'It is not simply that Sophia herself transforms, then, but that this transformation illustrates the lack of fixity of all received notions, and ideas of the self' (Baker 2019: 87).

Similarly, in the story 'A Stone Woman', A. S. Byatt uses transmogrifying becoming to challenge the protagonist's as well as the reader's expectations. Ines is a lexicographer who, after a stomach operation, turns to stones. The metonymic plural is an indication of the initial wrong assumption that Ines would die by petrification: 'she assumed it would end with the petrification of her vital functions' (2004a: 121). Turning to stones instead means becoming full of life. Ines is compared to a volcano: 'her veins were full of molten lava', 'she may erupt' (134), 'the red-hot liquid boil a little in her belly, in her lungs' (143). The shift that occurs in the story and that parallels the shape-shifting of the character redistributes the traditional hierarchical divides between *zoe* and *bios*, epistemology and ontology, subject and object, body and mind.

Ines transforms from the scientific observer and the object of study to the embodied experiencing subject. Indeed, at first, Ines is convinced that she is going to die and decides to record her strange metamorphosis for posterity: 'Then when "they" found her, "they" would have a record of how she had become what she was. She would observe, unflinching' (121). In keeping with her job description, she researches the stones that sprout haphazardly on her body in order to make sense of her transformation through the ordering classification of taxonomy. She looks at her body from a distance as she would an object of study, thus imitating the 'disembodied scientific objectivity' (Haraway 1988: 576) that 'se[es] everything from nowhere' (Haraway 1988: 581).

This approach is designated in the text as masculinist as it parallels allusions that equate the metamorphosis with the taboos associated with the female body. The transformation happens soon after the death of Ines's mother and the operation she undergoes reconstructs her navel, thus referring to the female sex as the origin of life. Ines's gangrenous guts are described like the pains of labour: 'pain struck her like a sudden beak, tearing at her gut. [. . .] It did not pass, but strengthened, blow on blow. She rolled on her bed, dishevelled and sweating. She heard the creature moaning' (112). She does not want to look at the scar with 'the sewed up lips of the hole' (113) that looks like a C-section wound: 'the wound was livid and ridged and ran the length of her white front, from under the ribs to the hidden places underneath her' (114–15). Ines is terrified and ashamed of the wound, 'she felt a kind of horror and shame looking at herself' (118), which she calls the blemish. Its many shades of red recall menstruation with 'her underwear appear[ing] to be catching threads' (118). Ines's tentative fingering of the wound is also reminiscent of the taboo of female masturbation: 'she explored the area tentatively with her fingertips over the cotton of her knickers' (118).

By defying her expectations, Ines's body also throws her scientific phallocentric frames of reference. She starts to appropriate the blemish through wonder: 'There were, increasingly, days when a new curiosity jostled the horror. One day, one of the blue veins on her inner thigh erupted into a line of rubious spinels, and she thought of jewels before she thought of pustules' (120). Becoming non-human reconciles Ines with her human female body. She also has a male helper, the Icelandic sculptor Thorsteinn.

The story of Ines and Thorsteinn also rewrites the phallocentric tale of Pygmalion from Ovid's *Metamorphoses*. While Pygmalion exemplifies the male power of creative genius that imitates the produce of nature – *natura naturata* – so powerfully that it comes to life, Ines's acceptance of her body, helped by the careful sculpting of serene Thorsteinn, emphasizes the inventiveness of nature itself – *natura naturans*. Jane Bennett uses the Spinozist distinction between *natura naturata* and *natura naturans* to contrast opposite conceptions of nature as 'brute matter' or as 'generativity' (2010: 117). Pygmalion is working anthropocentrically with brute matter that the human transforms through art. Thorsteinn is working anthropomorphically by 'look[ing] for the life in them [stones]' (132) and carving body parts like 'minuscule faces' or 'tiny bodies' whose unbelonging nevertheless makes them part of the stones: '[he] embellished them with forms of life that were alien and contradictory, yet part of them' (132). He helps Ines come to new life: he will take her to Iceland, the land of the trolls whom she will eventually join. He marvels at the fact that she is 'grown, not crafted' (135), the sprouting stones on her body testifying to 'the experiences in which the ego-bound human organism is experienced as the host of life-processes which it does not control and which carry on ruthlessly and regardlessly, [and] expresses the life of *zoe*' (Braidotti 2002: 132–3).

Byatt uses anthropomorphism to challenge anthropocentrism by drawing what Jane Bennett calls 'isomorphisms':

> A touch of anthropomorphism, then, can catalyze a sensibility that finds a world filled not with ontologically distinct categories of beings (subjects and objects) but with variously composed materialities that form confederations. In revealing similarities across categorical divides and lighting structural parallels between material forms in 'nature' and those in 'culture', anthropomorphism can reveal isomorphisms. (Bennett 2010: 99)

With her lexicographer character, Byatt reinterprets taxonomies. The classifying process inherited from the eighteenth century signals the superiority of the human mind in ordering nature through anthropocentric metaphors. Instead Byatt uses the diffractions of metonymic morphemes in scientific etymologies to sketch anthropomorphic proximities *in lieu of* divisions:

> The human world of stones is caught in organic metaphors like flies in amber. Words came from flesh and hair and plants. Reniform,

mammilated, botryoidal, dendrite, haematite. Carnelian is from carnal, from flesh. Serpentine and lizardite are stone reptiles; phyllite is leaf-green. The earth itself is made in part of bones, shells, diatoms. Ines was returning to it in a form quite different from her mother's fiery ash and bonemeal. She preferred the parts of her body that were now volcanic glasses, not bony chalk. Chabazite, from the Greek for hailstones, obsidian, which, like analcime and garnet, has the perfect icositetrahedral shape. (Byatt 2004a: 126–7)

Whereas the anthropocentric 'human world of stones' is fixed in the metaphoric process, Byatt's metonymic unravelling, encouraging the reader, through the example of Ines, to go look for themselves for the organic connections – 'reniform' refers to kidneys, 'mammilated' to breasts, 'botryoidal' to grapes, 'dendrite' to trees, 'haematite' to blood, 'garnet' to pomegranates – undoes the initial anthropocentric naming gesture to emphasize the enmeshment of the body with organic and inorganic matter, thus giving shape to equality: 'isomorphism'. That Byatt calls on the geometric modelling of the world – 'icositetrahedral' – also calls to mind Bennett. Instead of making the world intelligible – *bios* – Byatt's poetic process aims at defamiliarizing language through science. The strange signifieds, that the reader is hard put to pronounce correctly, thus also upsetting the signifiers, look like grotesque sculptures, just like Ines. When deciphering the lists of scientific words, the reader experiences the same puzzlement as Ines when her gaze becomes increasingly inhuman: 'her new eyes could not quite bring the dancing black letters to have any more meaning than the spiders and ants which scurried round her feet' (150). The experience materializes Byatt's belief that words are things. With 'A Stone Woman', she delivers what Jane Bennett calls an 'onto-story' to paint the fact that 'an affective, speaking human body is not radically different from the affective, signaling nonhumans with which it coexists, hosts, enjoys, serves, consumes, produces, and competes' (Bennett 2010: 117).

She went even further in her latest short story, 'Sea Story', by delivering the onto-story of a Perrier bottle. While the text starts with the 'painfully ordinary' (2013) human story of Harold, delivering the standard biography of a family triad and painting the familiar tale of love at first sight, it then unexpectedly turns its focus on the ocean journey of a plastic bottle. The strategy yet again serves to upset the reader's beliefs by contrasting Harold's romantic view of the sea as 'inhuman' (2013), along with his misreading of his first love Laura as a fairy-tale sea creature, with the larger picture of the marine extinction wrought by man-made items. The story plays with situational irony that opposes intent and result. Harold throws the Perrier bottle at sea with a love letter but the message that biologist Laura receives 'under her microscope' is that of 'the human occupation and corruption of the masterless ocean' (2013).

While Harold's mother used to write 'fierce little poems about waves and weather', student of literature Harold can only recycle clichés as he uses stanzas from Robert Burns's 'Red, Red Rose' that has become a cultural commodity commonly found on Valentine's cards. The addressee of Byatt's message, the contemporary reader concerned with climate change, however focuses on the poem's lines about the seas going dry and the melting rocks. Byatt reinterprets Burns's original intent of pitting Scottish dialect against the standard English emblematic of British imperialism from a non-anthropocentric perspective that contrasts fragile ecosystems and the Trash vortex. This ironic cultural recycling is echoed in the use of the registered trademark Perrier, a company that both commodifies and pollutes water. The parallel drawn between the objectification of women and of water is enhanced by the narrative of the non-human container.

The plastic material is depicted as taking on animal properties with 'its walls furring and feathering' (2013) that deceive the sea creatures into believing it is edible matter. Byatt's narrative pictures the agency of inorganic matter with the 'sumps of the world's washing machines' becoming 'silt', the toothbrushes forming 'shoals'. The sibilance of the 's' and 'sh' sounds emphasizes the porosity of the boundaries between inorganic garbage and organic life, thus outlining what Jane Bennett calls 'thing-power':

> an actant is neither an object nor a subject but an 'intervener' [...] An operator is that which, by virtue of its particular location in an assemblage and the fortuity of being in the right place at the right time, makes the difference, makes things happen, becomes the decisive force catalyzing an event. (Bennett 2010: 9)

The chain of consequences exemplified by the journey of a single Perrier bottle, killing in turns a mollymawk, a green turtle and a hagfish, serves to illustrate the 'intra-actions' between humans and non-humans, organic and inorganic matter. The dizzying web of connections is illustrated by the ekphrastic description of the Trash vortex as a 'pop painting': 'the crustaceans, copepods and fingerling fish that composed the brit are being replaced, little by little, by nurdles, the tiny plastic spheres made by manufactured microbeads of polyethylene thermoplastic, or by rubbed fragments of plastic debris, poetically known as mermaids' tears' (2013). The story was inspired by a discarded metaphor from *Ragnarok* that Byatt mentions in the concluding chapter-essay of her novel:

> When I began working on this story [*Ragnarok*] I had a metaphor in mind – I saw the death-ship Naglfar, made of dead men's nails, as an image for what is now known as the trash vortex, the wheeling collection of indestructible plastic in the Pacific [...] But I wanted to tell the myth in its own terms. (2011a: 168)

In 'Sea Story', the ekphrastic dimension of the depictions of destruction poetically recycles a scientific lexicon meant to capture at one and the same time the reality of extinction wrought by the fragmentation of particles forming a gyre – 'nurdles, microbeads of polyethylene thermoplastic' – and the beautiful biodiversity of marine ecology –

'the crustaceans, copepods and fingerling fish'. Byatt uses the non-human to shed light on human contradictions and conundrums such as that of well-meaning Harold who ends up polluting the ocean he loves to serve his deluded egotistic human love interest.

Similarly in *Ragnarok*, the retelling of the myth that parallels the realist story of the 'thin child' uses the inhuman god characters to portray human quandaries. The serpent Jörmungandr delights in destruction: '[she] loves to see the fish she kills and consumes, or indeed kills for fun, the coral she crushes and bleaches' (2011a: 168). Her father is the trickster god Loki whom Byatt paints as a zoologist: 'if I were writing an allegory, [. . .] [he] would be the detached scientific intelligence which could either save the earth or contribute to its rapid disintegration' (170–1). The serpent's hunger is expressed using ekphrastic taxonomic lists that mirror her greedy gluttony with the catalogue of taxa whetting her appetite and the many hues and colours promising a feast of textures: 'everything was abundant. Sponges, anemones, worms, crayfish, snails of every colour, ruby, chalky, jet, butter-yellow, sea slugs magnificently striped and mottled, supping up jelly from the fronds. Abalone were anchored round the holdfast, throngs of the shells in pink, red, green and the most succulent white' (67–8). This parallels the scene when the thin child crushes the buds of wild poppies:

> Then with her fingers she would prise open the petal-case apart, and extract the red, crumpled silk – slightly damp she thought – and spread it out in the sunlight. She knew in her heart she should not do this. She was cutting a life short, interrupting a natural unfolding, for the pleasure of satisfied curiosity and the glimpse of the secret, scarlet, creased and frilly flower-flesh. (36)

The sexual undertones of the passage once again invite a comparison between the spoliation of nature and the violation of the female sex while outlining the intrinsic invasiveness of scientific observation. The thin child however lived at a time when the world's riches were abundant, 'there were always more, so many more' (36) while the author currently inhabits a planet where life forms are dwindling: 'Every day I read of a new extinction, of the bleaching of the coral, and the disappearance of the codfish the thin child caught in the North Sea with a hook and line, when there were always more' (167). What Byatt aimed to figure with the non-human figures of greedy Jörmungandr and mischievous clever Loki were the human traits she sees as accounting for the end of her childhood's world: 'We are a species of animal which is bringing about the end of the world we were born into. Not out of evil or malice, or not mainly, but because of a lopsided mixture of extraordinary cleverness, extraordinary greed, extraordinary proliferation of our own kind, and a biologically built-in short-sightedness' (2011a: 167).

In *Ragnarok*, Byatt contrasts a perspective on the world as resources and food with the insatiable serpent and as nourishment with the thin child's sustenance through books. Indeed *Ragnarok* was conceived as a homage to Byatt's mother, to whom the book is dedicated, through a rewriting of the book *Asgard and the Gods* adapted from Wagner by M. W. McDowal that belonged to her. The chapters in *Ragnarok* are headed with reproductions of the original engravings. This early passion for books is echoed in the final bibliography the author includes. Byatt takes a moral stance here to demonstrate the agency of books in the world by weaving her own childhood body experiences – including that of asthma which her evacuation to the countryside during the blackout cured – with her delight in the words of botany and in the world of the Asgard gods. In the text she also references Darwin's 'tangled bank' and Bunyan's *The Pilgrim's Progress*, while the bibliography mentions scientific sources on botany, marine ecology, extinction and chaos theory.

Corine Pelluchon has developed what she calls 'a philosophy of living from' to argue for a new social contract based on an eco-phenomenology. She pits the notion of nourishment against that of food to go beyond the dualism of nature and culture:

> Indeed nourishment does not appear all on its own: it requires other people's work and poses the problem of sharing with other human beings and other species. Justice, the fact that our way of inhabiting the earth and of preserving its beauty pertains to ethics and politics, as well as the importance that nourishment has for us when we take pleasure in it – or when the destruction of it also harms us intimately, as if 'the world is one's body' – implies that fields that are ordinarily separated, such as morality, politics, ecology, and aesthetics, are integrated within a philosophy of existence and with its underlying ontology. (2019: 14)

It is my contention that women writers are currently reworking realist writing to precisely transcend the boundaries between science, literature, morality and politics to foster new post-anthropocentric imaginings of human becomings. Why realism? Because of its tradition of engaging both scientifically and empirically with descriptions of the world. Why women? Because of their own embodied experience that their critical writing transforms into a process of becoming minoritarian. With the help of feminism, especially a feminist epistemology of science, they rewrite the naturalist novel that Zola theorized as an experimental novel.

Referring to the physiologist Claude Bernard and his experimental method in medicine, Zola defined the naturalist writer as a scientist experimenting with his characters as phenomena in a complex social environment. Hall's survivalist strategies designed to test the limits of her characters can be paralleled with Zola's experimental method. Zola quotes from Bernard to draw the contours of the naturalist novel: 'there is no longer either materialism, or spiritualism, or inanimate matter, or living matter; there remain but phenomena' (1893: 30). Such an idea strikes one as congruent with Karen Barad's agential realism as the study of the intra-actions between material-discursive forces. There are no objects as such except as materialized phenomena.

Zola and Bernard, however, writing within the nineteenth century's anthropocentric paradigm, aimed at conquering through knowledge: 'to study phenomena in order to become their master' (1893: 24). From that perspective, the morality advocated by Zola – who compares the experimentalist to 'the examining magistrate of nature' and the experimental novelist to 'the examining magistrate of men and their passions' (1893: 10) – is to cure the social ills by handing over to the legislator the study of their phenomena. Again, there is a similarity with the justice movement that inspires the new material feminist work of Alaimo, Barad, Haraway or Neimanis. Hall uniquely mobilizes the judicial question in her novels, and her latest collection of short stories, *Sudden Traveller*, features as its opening story that of a female avenger. In 'M', a female lawyer turns into a harpy to abort the victims of rape and punish the perpetrators.

The difference is that this call for justice relies on a post-anthropocentric change of paradigm effected by the feminist epistemology of science: the divides between subjects and objects, nature and culture, no longer stand. Literary naturalism gets redefined. Whereas Zola drew a parallel between the experimental science of medicine as the study of nature and novel writing as the 'practical sociology' (1893: 26) of human nature, the current reformulation of disciplinary boundaries re-entangles the so-called natural bodies with their social habits and habitats in the nature-culture continuum. Morality no longer concerns social ills but enlarges itself to the reciprocal comprehension of human embodiment within environmental embeddedness. Literature as nourishment participates in this justice movement that calls for a recognition of the variety of 'actants' – including books – that shape the world we live in and form. The pleasure of the serpent, which merges with the pleasure of Byatt in ekphrasizing taxonomy, in appropriating hedonically the words of science, encourage the reader to 'discover a gourmet ego, which is also a gourmet cogito, for which need is not primarily a care for existence, but a need of nourishment that includes at once the pleasure taken in nourishment' (Pelluchon 2019: 32).

The specific phenomenology of Byatt's writing is to infuse science with pleasure, to map out sensorially the botanical, zoological, entomological depictions of the world. In the entomological novella 'Morpho Eugenia', from the 1992 collection *Angels and Insects*, Byatt rewrites the myth of Oedipus and its psychoanalytical reading to morph anthropocentric science into posthuman analogical identities and differences. The story told from the point of view of William Adamson is that of an eye opener on the incestuous relationship between his wife and her brother. It is revealed to him through the scrambled letters of a game of Anagrams by the governess Matty Compton who turns the word 'insect' into the word 'incest'. Matty also writes the embedded tale, 'Things Are Not What They Seem', in which a human turned into an insect must solve the sphynx's puzzle to recover his human form. The sphynx however is not the lion-headed woman from the myth, but the moth, Sphinx Acherontia Atropos, named by Linnaeus. While the answer to the riddle in the myth is 'man', in Byatt's tale, the character must name the sphynx and the answer is 'kind'. Byatt uses insect and incestuous analogies between kinds to turn the anthropocentric and phallocentric world view of William Adamson upside down. She has written in *On Histories and Stories*: 'I see insects as the Not-human, in some sense the Other, and I believe we ought to think about the not-human, in order to be fully human. Insects are the objects of much anthropomorphising attention' (2001b: 115). By morphing the mythological chimera sphynx into its entomological material counterpart, the hawkmoth species, Byatt mocks the Freudian myth that resulted in mythologizing the feminine as monstrous. By naturalizing the riddle, she de-centres the human.

Using anthropomorphizing analogies in this novella allows Byatt to go beyond gender and use kind to devise trans-species mutations in a way that heralds Braidotti's 'becoming animal': 'They [the insects] pose the question of radical otherness not in metaphorical but in bio-morphic terms, that is to say as a metamorphosis of the sensory and cognitive apparatus' (Braidotti 2002: 149). Byatt turns the reader into a parataxonomist collaborator who, like William Adamson himself, will endeavour to decipher the clues in the etymological scrambles. Thus the maiden name of William's wife, Alabaster, refers to a perfume vase, from the Greek *alabastros*, recalling the metaphor of the female body as a vessel, but also to the Egyptian goddess, Bastet, represented as a lioness. The first name 'Eugenia' refers to the eugenics of Francis Galton while the title of the novella references the lepidoptera named after the Empress Eugénie. Morpho means shape and is also one of the names of Aphrodite. The humans turning into animals in Matty's tale echo the taxonomic mutations of animals into mythological or historical figures. Byatt portrays the entanglements of the human and the non-human through lexical genetics that keep spawning analogical knots. Byatt's kinds are equal to Haraway's 'making kin', unexpected connections that change the Oedipal story of family ties:

> My purpose is to make 'kin' mean something other/more than entities tied by ancestry or genealogy. [. . .] Kin-making is making persons, not necessarily as individuals or as humans. I was moved in college by Shakespeare's punning between kin and kind – the kindest were not necessarily kin as family; making kin and making kind (as category, care, relatives without ties by birth, lateral relatives, lots of other echoes). Marylin Strathern taught me that relatives in British English were originally 'logical relations' and only became 'family members' in the 17th century [. . .]
>
> I think that the stretch and recomposition of kin are allowed by the fact [that] all earthlings are kin in the deepest sense, and it is past time to practice better care of kinds-as-assemblages (not species one at a time). Kin is an assembling sort of word. All critters share a common 'flesh,' laterally, semiotically, and genealogically. Ancestors turn out to be very interesting strangers; kin are unfamiliar (outside what we thought was family or genes), uncanny, haunting active. (Haraway 2015: 161–2)

Byatt's gourmet writing about science materializes making kinds as assemblages. Her latest short story, 'Sea Story', testifies to her growing concern with ekphrasizing the common flesh of the world.

Sarah Hall could be said to make skin. Her writing offers 'a phenomenology of the skin, our susceptibility or our permeability to the world' (Pelluchon 2019: 38). She dedicated her second novel from 2004, *The Electric Michelangelo*, to tattoo art. Her border writing materializes the porosity of the frontier between bodies, most dramatically when women are being forced, most poetically when they become other. Hall contrasts a phallocentric notion of the border as a site of violation with a post-anthropocentric understanding of it as a spatialized moment of transferences. The skin and bones of her characters harbour wild life, like Janet's whose 'collarbones had deep shadows and in them hung the carcasses of animals in the savannah' (Hall 2016a: 250) while their bodies are forged by seasonal weather patterns, 'her body chemistry alters as the terrain decomposes, turns, begins again' (Hall 2016a: 112). The animal comparisons that abound in her novels are always a surprise as they are not determined by what Braidotti calls 'oedipalized relations' (Braidotti 2009), that is a hierarchy that equates biological features with moral values, but rather by anthropomorphic analogies that descry equal shapes, or isomorphisms, between humans and animals. Janet's face is that of a leopard, 'taut' (2016: 81), surveying her native land with a hunter's gaze. The colour red equates the character's heart with the fox in 'Bees'. In *The Wolf Border*, Rachel is compared to a she-wolf. Although no transmogrification takes place, she cannot but evoke the imaginary of Angela Carter and her Wolf Alice. Rosi Braidotti calls on Angela Carter to characterize this 'process of trans-species nomadism' in which the '"explosion" of the civilized confines of one's "self" re-asserts some raw corporeality of the subject' (Braidotti 2002: 128).

A new imaginary of 'enfleshed materialism' (Braidotti 2002: 137) is being developed by women writers calling on a critical positioning of radical immanence converting female embodiment into a transformative empowering process. The fact that this enfleshed materialism also colours their realistic writing is all the more relevant as it means to transcribe a paradigmatic change in the perception of reality derived from empirical experience: new descriptions of the world are needed to further a post-anthropocentric understanding of the human.

7

The new realist imaginary

It matters to offer new readings of realism today at a time when reality itself is fast changing in a world affected by global pandemics. This was precisely the subject of Sarah Moss's first novel from 2009 *Cold Earth*. This polyphonic speculative realist novel narrates an archaeological expedition to Greenland turning to disaster with the threat of a global pandemic shutting the explorers off from the world as they lose their means of communication. Six characters successively unveil the chronological chain of events using second-person narratives that turn out to be what they believe are their last words to loved ones. The narrative strategy used by Moss accentuates the claustrophobic sense of isolation and panic. On her website, Moss wrote about her source of inspiration and a strange coincidence: 'I was thinking of avian flu while I wrote the early drafts, but the WHO – rather disconcertingly – declared swine flu to be a global pandemic on the day of publication'. Her latest novel from 2018, *Ghost Wall*, also uses archaeology as a background to fictionalize group behaviours.

In *Cold Earth*, the challenge of a rising panic drives major rifts in the group with Nina's ghost-seeing materializing the contagion of fear in the small-scale community, while Yanni, the head of the expedition, dies from his voluntary isolation from the group when he decides to save the findings of the digs against the better collective judgement. *Ghost Wall* uses an experiential archaeological summer camp in Northumberland to tackle the themes of British nationalism, domestic abuse and collective denial that come to a head with the final scapegoating of the first-person narrator Silvie. Her father Bill is a nationalist bus driver and amateur archaeologist who has been invited to join the experience for his survivalist skills. His ill-treatment of Silvie and her mother contaminates the group as the male members, playing at hunting, decide to re-enact the ritual sacrifice of a teenage girl and get carried away to the sound of drum beats. The familial abuse mirrors the national situation and the xenophobic scapegoating promoted by Brexit supporters. By contrast the archaeological context exposes the myth of Britishness by recalling the presence of the Romans who were not even Romans themselves but Syrian and German. This was also Bernardine Evaristo's purpose in *The Emperor's Babe* and *Soul Tourists*.

Realist women writers today are appropriating the Brexit nationalist context to draw parallels between xenophobia and women's abuse through scapegoating. This is also the case in Melissa Harrison's 2018 *All Among the Barley*. Set in rural East Anglia in 1933, the novel parallels the dramatic situation of farmers at the time of the Depression and the rise of fascism in England with Oswald Mosley and the British Union of Fascists. The first-person narrator, the teenage girl Edie, is beguiled by the figure of emancipated woman and Londoner journalist Constance Fitzallen who turns out to have a political agenda and comes to the village to spread fascist ideas based on the idyll of rural Britishness. The daughter of a Pakistani mother, Harrison explained how she wrote the novel with a view to 'question that picture' of 'Deep England' as 'an almost pre-lapsarian, highly exclusive vision that is south-eastern, middle-class, Anglican and white' (Harrison 2018b).

The current development of post-pastoral literature exemplified by such writers as Sarah Hall, Sarah Moss or Melissa Harrison testifies to an environmental appropriation of the geopolitical spaces of rural

England. Sarah Hall's novels contrast an anthropocentric approach to the land as systemized by regulations, pre-empted by governing bodies, owned and exploited by a few privileged, annexed and mapped out by the military, with a pragmatic post-pastoral perspective that weaves together the intra-actions of human labour, geological forces, animal life and weather patterns. Terry Gifford has identified six characteristic features of post-pastoral writing:

> awe leading to humility in the face of the destructive-creative forces of nature; awareness of the culturally loaded language we use about the country; accepting responsibility for our relationship with nature and its dilemmas; recognition that the exploitation of nature is often accompanied by the exploitation of the less powerful people who work with it, visit it or less obviously depend on its resources. (44)

Post-pastoral writing is posthuman in that it redefines a world-in-common based on reciprocal exposure rather than on taxonomic hierarchies ordering the world from a human perspective cataloguing resources and risks. History is used differently than it was in the 1990s historiographic metafictions. By embedding the historical stratum in the embodied experience of their characters and in the local terrain, writers ontologize time as matter. Whereas historiographic metafictions like Byatt's *Possession* problematized the epistemological dimension of both historical and literary narratives, the novels of those millennial writers focus on the empirical experience of resurgence, which accounts for the anachronisms in Hall's *Haweswater* of the extinct golden eagle and the references to the death camps. Sarah Moss's second novel, *Night Waking*, brought up the unresolved death of a nineteenth-century baby in the contemporary setting of a remote Scottish island reminiscent of St Kilda. It inspired Moss to write two historical novels, *Bodies of Light* and *Signs for Lost Children*, that pursue the storyline of nineteenth-century child mortality while tackling the rise of English feminism, medicine and mental health, and British imperialism.

When opting for first-person accounts like Moss's *Ghost Wall* and Harrison's *All Among the Barley*, the immersion into the characters' confused world view helps raise onto-epistemic issues of situated knowledges. Very often they are not easy characters to read with, which serves to highlight ethical conundrums. Silvie in *Ghost Wall* cannot but defend her father to the friend who would help her, refusing to acknowledge his abuse, ultimately consenting to her own murder before the group is finally stopped. Her mother, likewise, keeps insisting she willingly plays the role of the camp's cook and housewife and urges her daughter to not anger her father. The group as a whole turns a blind eye to his violence so that it spirals into a collective sacrificial ritual. The novel aptly raises the questions of collective denial and complicity that the Me Too movement helped bring to the fore. Edie in *All Among the Barley* is quite young, which accounts for her blindness to Constance's agenda. She ends up spending her life at a mental health hospital after being raped.

It is no wonder then that in the fiction of these women writers, most notably Sarah Hall's, legal and judicial issues keep surfacing to question power versus empowerment. Moss's *Night Waking* refers to the Highland Clearances which evicted the farming tenants to create large-scale pastoral farms and led to the creation of the crofting communities. This changed with the 2003 Land Reform carried out in Scotland, which Hall's *The Wolf Border* alludes to. Harrison's novels *At Hawthorne Time* and *All Among the Barley* raise the issue of trespassing, with the quaint figure of Jack, the agricultural traveller in *At Hawthorne Time*, and the Jewish family occupying an empty house in *All Among the Barley*. Land rights figure prominently in post-pastoral literature and are paralleled with minority rights, thus raising the question of what we collectively share and how we collectively care.

The parallel between awareness of environmental interdependence and justice claims is similar to that developed by posthuman philosophy. Writers are experimenting with personal pronouns, especially with the unusual second person, to encourage the reader to actively participate in a collective interrogation about shared feelings and how they could move one to action through care. In her new collection of short stories, Sarah Hall has again used a second-person narrator in 'Sudden Traveller' which gives its title to the collection. As in 'Bees', the second person translates the state of shock the narrator is in. She has just lost her mother, whose cancer was diagnosed at the time when the narrator was expecting her first child. She is weaning her baby at the same time as she buries her mother while the country is on lockdown because of floods. The state of dissociation marked by the second person also offers a way towards the second-person plural which calls on the readers to share grief: 'You will begin to understand that those who suffer, suffer the same. In this condition, we are never alone' (Hall 2019: 110). The second-person plural explains the story's title and gives it the universal dimension of what a human life amounts to: 'We are, all of us, sudden travellers in the world, blind, passing each other, reaching out, missing, sometimes taking hold' (110).

In her collection of short stories published in 2019, Zadie Smith has also experimented with the second-person plural in 'The Lazy River'. The story, set in a holiday resort in Spain, interrogates our sense of communality by looking for similarities despite differences. Thus the collective pronoun 'we' keeps changing, wavering between universality and identitarian markers. The first sentence reads as a universal statement which sounds like a warning: 'We're submerged, all of us' (Smith 2019a: 25). Soon after, the pronoun turns out to designate the British as the story is revealed as a Brexit story. First published in *The New Yorker* in 2017, the text refers to that same year when the country's withdrawal became official in March. Although the text introduces differences between the British compatriots in terms of social classes, characterizing in particular an elite who voted to remain in the EU, it points out how all of them are still going to end up in the same river: 'they will climb back into the metaphor with the rest, back into this watery Ouroboros, which, unlike the river of Heraclitus, is always the same no matter where you happen to step in it' (28).

The split in the pronouns that marks both similarities and differences is echoed in the literal metaphor that guides the story. Like the pronouns that keep switching from universality to social hierarchy, so the metaphor is and is not a metaphor: 'The Lazy River is a metaphor and at the same time a real body of artificial water' (26). Smith twice refers to Heraclitus in the story, quoting his paradox: '"We both step and do not step in the same rivers. We are and are not." So said Heraclitus' (30). Using the Greek philosopher, Smith applies the same idea to the metaphor. Metaphor is built on difference, not similarity. In the text, the literal meaning constantly resurfaces so the metaphoric meaning never completely separates from its literal source. Smith constantly accommodates difference and similarity at one and the same time.

Similarly the first person is both Zadie Smith herself and an anonymous narrator, just as the second-person singular is sometimes her husband and sometimes the readers. Following the opening sentence, the text reads 'all of us. You, me, the children' (25) referencing the writer's family while later on the 'we' of the family unit describes their education principles: '[we] divert our children's eyes from the obscene bulge of those iPhones, the existence of which we have decided not to reveal to them for many years, or at least until they are twelve' (33). They are described as belonging with the elite previously characterized in the text as minding their children's diet and exposure to the sun. However the writer aims to remain non-judgemental as when she freely confesses to having peed in the pool like everyone else. She is and is not 'we'. She is and is not Zadie Smith.

The story is also a story about climate change. The split pronouns and the metaphor-not-metaphor build towards an understanding of the nature-cultures we live in. While referencing such environmental issues as plastic pollution, intensive farming, overfishing, global warming, mass tourism and waste management, the story questions the natural/artificial divide. The tomatoes are artificially grown, the teenage girls on the beach work hard to artificially shoot natural-looking poses, the Spanish sun offers a perfect tan while also threatening with cancer, the chemicals in the swimming river are meant to make it look naturally blue while the urine reveals the artificiality of the chlorine:

> No, the sad consequence of the green is that it concentrates the mind in a very unpleasant way upon the fundamental artificiality of the Lazy River. Suddenly what had seemed quite natural – floating slowly in an unending circle, while listening to the hit of the summer, which itself happens to be called 'Slowly' – seems not only unnatural but surpassingly odd. Less like a holiday from life than like some kind of terrible metaphor for it. (29)

The universal-differentiated 'we' and the metaphor-not-metaphor work together in the text to reach beyond binary oppositions and offer instead a hyphenated version of how everything connects. Ultimately the story asks the question: 'What is the solution to life? How can it be lived "well"?' (29). The narrator's interrogation is repeated by the Gambian migrant woman braiding hair on the beach: '"To live well?" Cynthia adds, pulling our daughter's hair, making her yelp. "Is not easy."' (33) The Brexit story that alerts to dividing the British community from the rest of the EU on account of a further rejection of migrant workers begs the question of what we have in common beyond our individual circumstances or identitarian markers. The climate change story further calls on our collective responsibility towards the world: we all pee in the pool, how come it falls to the janitor to 'clean whatever scum we have left of ourselves off the sides' (34)?

This is the last sentence of the text. It encourages the readers to reflect on their own routines and habits of thought: the social hierarchy that would place the janitor at the bottom rung of the ladder reveals the inconsequential praxis of the privileged with not a care in the world while on a 'getaway' from their daily life in a Spanish resort.

How to re-appropriate the everyday as a site for acknowledging collective and individual accountability? This is why realism matters: it is about ordinary quotidian lives that have become burdened with unprecedented material repercussions with the advent of the Anthropocene. Our daily routines are also the answer to those unparalleled changes, providing a local site from which to observe global phenomena. This may account for the turn to phenomenological first-person narratives cast in the form of the essay. In 2016, Melissa Harrison published *Rain. Four Walks in English Weather.* It was jointly published by the National Trust and Faber & Faber after they struck a deal in 2014 to publish narrative non-fiction. In this essay, Harrison depicts rain as a 'co-author' (2016a: xiii) modifying the landscape through erosion but also transforming it perceptually: 'changing how the English countryside looks, smells, and sounds' (xiii). This sensory apprehension guides the construction of the book divided in four seasonal walks through four regions of England. In addition to the phenomenological narrative of first-person weather experience, Harrison includes meteorological and topographic data, historical reminders of hydraulic and agricultural developments, human specific habits and habitats in relation to watery places, naturalist observations on wild life and weather with references to previous nature writing texts (Joseph Taylor, Alfred Wainwright), recent scientific studies and citizen science endeavours like the British Rainfall Organization (32–3), a final lexicon of local rain-related terms and expressions from all over England as well as a glossary of meteorological terms and a bibliography. The book is illustrated with black and white engravings by Paul Binnie.

This combination of scientific facts and observations with the empirical experience of the narrator registering the sensory alterations authored by rain could be likened to the 'concept-creation' of weathering called forth by Neimanis and Walker (2014: 560). Their concept aims to modify the dissociated apprehension of climate change as too large and too complex to comprehend by 'help[ing] gestate [a] new imaginary' (2014: 560) that calls on personal experience and sensations. Harrison clearly outlines how she means to re-imagine England not as the pastoral myth used by nationalist ideologues but as a post-pastoral tale of weathering: 'This book does not pretend to be an exhaustive survey of the country's natural history during precipitation, and nor is it a purely scientific investigation into a meteorological phenomenon; instead, it's an imaginative account of how England – human, animal and vegetable – weathers, and is weathered, by the storm' (xv).

Harrison's impulse to write the book issued forth from the idea to bear witness to what happens outdoors when it rains while most of us seek refuge indoors: 'Because it's something that sends most of us scurrying indoors, few people witness what actually happens out in the landscape on a wet afternoon' (xiii). This is related to the parallel Neimanis and Walker draw between our dissociation from climate change and our comfortable way of life: 'if climate change is an abstract notion, this is closely bound to a privileged Western life that is committed to keeping the weather out' (2014: 561). The book turns the picture postcard icon of English identity – rain – into a potential for new thinkings and new becomings. In the epilogue, Harrison explains that the experience has changed her for the better: 'My year of getting wet – and thinking about, and reading about, rain – has broadened and deepened my feeling for the outside world. I'm no longer just a fair-weather walker; I can choose now to overcome the impulse for comfort and convenience that insulates us not only for the bad in life but from much of the good' (87).

Experiencing the weather physically allows Harrison to better understand her humanity by becoming animal: 'I think we need the weather, in all its forms, to feel fully human – which is to say, an animal' (87). Becoming animal, along the lines of Deleuze's and Braidotti's philosophies, means that 'thinking can be critical if by critical we mean the active, affirmative invention of new images of thought' (Braidotti 2009: 527). Turning to narrative non-fiction as an assemblage of history, literature and science, told in the phenomenological first-person, contributes to critically assess how weather and weathering may be felt and conceptualized at one and the same time today to address the tenuous distinction between climactic patterns – like the English temperate maritime climate – and weather events – like flash floods. As evidenced by the choice of seasonal walks, this is also a tale about spacetime. Weathering, in Neimanis and Walker's text, means that 'we seek to cultivate a sensibility that attunes us not only to the "now" of the weather, but toward ourselves and the world as weather bodies, mutually caught up in the whirlwind of a weather-world, in the thickness of climate-time' (2014: 561). By referencing the past endeavours at measuring rainfall, the agricultural changes to the landscape, the hydraulic systems from the Romans' aqueducts to today's reservoirs, the cloud variations, the erosion that sculpted the river beds and the rocks, alongside her own walks in the rain in waterproof gear, Harrison indeed criss-crosses human and non-human time frames that defy chronological succession in favour of constantly mutating phenomena in which her own body feels included.

A similar intent characterizes the seasons' anthologies that Harrison edited for the Wildlife Trusts in 2016. In them, Harrison has chosen to mix prose and poetry, texts by renowned writers and members of the general public, from all time periods and from all over England. In each introduction, she casts the anthology in relation to climate change in order to raise the readers' awareness at the same time as she encourages them to 'engage with nature physically, intellectually, and emotionally, rather than allow ourselves to disconnect; that we witness rather than turn away and celebrate rather than neglect' (2016b: x).

The growing interest in developing everyday awareness of global phenomena, in fictional and non-fictional forms, coupled with phenomenological experimentations with the first person and the collective second person, testifies to the relevance of literature in contributing to the public debate in a world faced with unparalleled changes. Why does realism matter? Because it allows people to connect their daily personal experience with that of others: 'one motive for reading is the hope of gaining a deeper sense of everyday experiences and the shape of social life' (Felski 2008: 83). This is also the point of Zadie Smith's article from 2019, 'Fascinated to Presume'. She quotes examples from Charlotte Brontë, Alice Walker, V. S. Naipaul and Charles Dickens to laud the capacity of the novel to promote empathy across a wide array of different eras, world views and experiences:

> And what I did in life, I did with books. I lived in them and felt them live in me. I felt I *was* Jane Eyre and Celie and Mr. Biswas and David Copperfield. Our autobiographical coordinates rarely matched. I'd never had a friend die of consumption or been raped by my father or lived in Trinidad or the Deep South or the nineteenth century. (Smith 2019b)

Reading creates imaginary communities beyond personal, national, racial, sexual circumstances. Those illegitimate communities, as Rancière calls them, are similar to the ones drawn by Stacy Alaimo on account of their exposure to toxicity in that they defy any traditional identity markers in favour of unexpected kinships: 'To occupy exposure as insurgent vulnerability is to perform material rather than abstract alliances, and to inhabit a fraught sense of political agency that emerges from the perceived loss of boundaries and sovereignty' (Alaimo 2016: 5). The novels of Sarah Hall can aptly be described as novels of exposure affiliating as they do female labourers, indigenous people, extinct species and landscapes. Bringing forth issues of land sovereignty and the porosity of physical boundaries – whether geographic, intimate, as in the many examples of ambiguous sexual congress, or speciesist – they map out new potentials for collective cooperation. Owning exposure is a feminist gesture. Re-describing reality today matters particularly to women writers engaged in a dialogue with the world.

Both Zadie Smith and A. S. Byatt identify curiosity as the driving force of their writing. For Byatt, scientific curiosity allows for an outward-looking re-description of reality motivated by wonder:

> For the Age of Suspicion led to solipsism, to navel-gazing, to a sense that the inside of our own head was all we could know. This complacent mental misery makes no sense in the world of scientific discovery. We need to feel that there is something real out there – of which we are a part and not the whole – and science reveals it to us in its beauty and its terror and its order and its chaos, bit by fascinating bit, cell by cell, gene by gene, galaxy by galaxy. (Byatt 2000b)

Wondering about the microscopic and macroscopic shapes of the world and wondering at their beauty blends feeling with knowledge. It sums up Byatt's latest endeavours at combining literature and science and it looks like she has found a way to overcome the body/mind dilemma of her first novels through writing that transcends the boundaries of disciplines. Like Haraway, she is a 'compostist' (Haraway 2015: 161). 'Sea Story' in particular reads as a compostist onto-story comparing short-lived organic matter with the life cycle of plastic waste. *Ragnarok* composts autobiography, myth, essay and taxonomic ekphrasis to problematize extinction.

Zadie Smith's focus is curiosity about people. Although she cannot be likened to a posthumanist, there is definitely a new materialist dimension to her writing in the way she characterizes books as actants that contribute to giving the readers more autonomy than the new technologies:

> This data version of you is 'correct' to the nth degree: it sees all and knows all, and makes the fuzzy knowledge of selves that fiction once claimed look truly pathetic. A book does not watch us reading it; it cannot morph itself, page by page, to suit our tastes, or deliver to us only depictions of people we already know and among whom we feel comfortable. It cannot note our reactions and then skew its stories to confirm our worldview or reinforce our prejudices. A book does not know when we pick it up and put it down; it cannot nudge us into the belief that we must look at it first thing upon waking and last thing at night, and though it may prove addictive, it will never know exactly how or why. (Smith 2019b)

She commends the unpredictability of a reader's relation to a book along with 'the fuzzy knowledge' of people provided by literature. To be affected or not by a book matters to the reader. To imagine yourself as someone else matters to the writer. This curiosity is also a form of wonder. However, like Byatt, Smith does not only wonder at people's idiosyncrasies but also wonders about their failures, their deceptions, their corruption, their pettiness in line with the great realist novels of the nineteenth century: 'And the strange thing is that the people we now cast into this place of non-interest were once the very people fiction was most curious about. The conflicted, the liars, the self-deceiving, the willfully blind, the abject, the unresolved, the imperfect, the evil, the unwell, the lost and divided. Those were once fiction's people' (Smith 2019b).

Like Barker and Tremain, Smith is interested in the imperfect humans abjected by society which lead to her controversial short story 'Now More Than Ever' published in the wake of the Me Too incriminations online. In the story, the first-person narrator is out of tune with the present-day call for consistency that would have the relation between past and present as a 'seamless' one (Smith 2019a:

226). Smith is adamant about the right to change your mind, to be wrong, to fail. In the foreword to her first collection of essays, *Changing My Mind*, she thus asserted that 'ideological inconsistency is, for me, practically an article of faith' (Smith 2011). The foreword also refers to a non-fictional book which she failed to produce entitled *Fail Better: The Morality of the Novel*, but which was published as an essay in *The Guardian* in 2007. The title is borrowed from Samuel Beckett's lines in 'Worstward Ho': 'Ever tried. Ever failed. No matter. Try again. Fail again. Fail better'. The failings of the characters are also those of the writer, the reader and the book itself. The parallel injunction in her essay is 'read better'. Reading better means understanding the writer's working mind, thus allowing to get tangled in another's viewpoint and deliberate with her about differences and commonalities, allowing to change one's mind, to be transformed by reading. This is consistent with Smith's call on Heraclitus in 'The Lazy River' and how everything is in flux.

In the cases of Barker, Levy and Tremain, the abject is also a way to engage the reader in a dialogue with the book as a mediator on what society and community mean. Just like Harrison and Moss posing difficult questions about group behaviour and fear as social contagion, so Barker's *Blow Your House Down* was explicitly a way to tackle collective guilt in femicides: 'It's a difficult book. It is complicit, but then I take that on board, because I think society is complicit, and we are part of that society' (Brannigan and Barker 2005b: 392). Barker evokes the difficult reception of the novel and how 'I'm glad I'm not a fly on the classroom wall in a lot of these classes, I think especially when they're teaching *Blow Your House Down*' (Brannigan and Barker 2005b: 392). Thus the realist novel can also engineer shock in its readers by exposing them to their own failings, contriving a moral crash rather than the aesthetic clash of the avant-garde:

> The ethos of the avant-garde claims shock as its ultimate weapon, a strategy for confounding and astounding the dim-witted

bourgeoisie, the credulous masses, the pompous prelates and guardians of culture. A clear line is drawn between insiders and outsiders, the insolent insurgents and the sadly unenlightened, those who shock and the hypocrites and charlatans who deserve to be shocked. Shock is seized as a source of symbolic advantage, a guarantee of oppositional purity or redemptive politics, shoring up the certitude of one's own advanced consciousness. It is, in short, eviscerated of any genuine terror. Yet it is also possible for shock to work in other ways: to blur the distinction between self and other, to unravel the certainty of one's own convictions rather than sustaining them. Shock in this sense is not a blithe herald of future freedom from all tyrannies and oppression but a graphic illustration of the internal as well as external obstacles that lie in the way of such freedom. (Felski 2008: 110)

Andrea Levy works with Felski's 'shock of recognition' (Felski 2008: 133) understood as redress: 'the seemingly rationalist idea of recognition turns out to rely on an interplay of sameness and difference, strangeness and familiarity: what the mirror shows us is not always what we hoped or expected to see' (Felski 2008: 133). Levy's prime motive for writing is to have the British Black history acknowledged. Her last book, *The Long Song*, in particular, was designed to tackle the difficult issue of slavery precisely because it is not being engaged with: 'There's a lot of guilt, and guilt causes people not to want to engage. And that is what the history of the Caribbean and the British Empire is about, it's about guilt and not engaging' (Rowell and Levy 2015: 270). To engage her readers, Levy chose the popular form of the realist novel because

> Having my audience is extremely important to me, because I have something that I want to express and share. So I'm not happy to just write a novel that sells to two or three thousand people who thought it was 'rather difficult' but they got through it. It doesn't interest me because there's a mission that I am on. That's about the history of the Caribbean, it's about black people in this country, it's

about raising awareness, and it's about the confrontation of people of color with the British Empire. (Rowell and Levy 2015: 277)

She owns the bestselling status of her novels as a means to get the story of British Black people out there. To address the shocking aspect of slavery, she relied on the everyday:

> 'When you try to imagine slavery in terms of what happened it's almost unthinkable,' she says. 'But people got through it. Not every day was: "Got up, got whipped thoroughly, saw someone hung from a tree". So I try to give a sense of the daily life – the drinking milk and eating yam of it – as well as the lives of the planter class. I try to give people their humanity.' (Younge and Levy 2010)

And she laced the tragic with the comic, as she did in her previous novels:

> It's funny. And then you start to acknowledge the real humanity in people. People then stop becoming just the victim of a tragedy. They become real people, and you can understand how their lives would have evolved. They become like you and me. And that's always what I try to do – so that anybody's who's reading my book would have – even though you have 200, 300 years separating you from a character – complete empathy, because you understand this person, the way they think – and you can't do that if they never give you something to smile about. (Baxter and James 2014: 137)

Working with humour as Levy, Evaristo, Tremain and Smith do invites the reader to engage with both sympathetic and antipathetic characters in an affective, personal relationship born of realist psychological verisimilitude. The everyday is instrumental in forging the relation on the basis of immersion whether in the familiar or the unfamiliar routine because 'the quotidian is not an objectively given quality but a lived relationship' (Felski 2000: 31). The very experience of reading a book is at one and the same time routine and a rupture of routine. This is the message behind Harrison's season anthologies:

the book is a companion that both attends cyclical time and testifies to the current fracture of what we thought was unalterable.

Realist literature matters in helping to reconcile ourselves to constant change, Heraclitus's flux, by anchoring the human in new and old routines. Tremain's novels often contrast characters stuck in the past whose physical ailments mirror a paralysis of the self with transmigrating characters on a journey of constant transition. This is most obviously the case in *Sacred Country* with many of its middle-aged male characters desperately holding onto an antiquated idea of England which manifests itself as a cancer, a palsy, a deaf ear, a hearing loss or else aphonia, while Mary/Martin journeys towards her/his reassignment. Routine as a lived relationship helps transitioning towards new embodiments and a new sense of embeddedness. As Arundhati Roy recently wrote about the coronavirus crisis, 'the pandemic is a portal':

> Historically, pandemics have forced humans to break with the past and imagine their world anew. This one is no different. It is a portal, a gateway between one world and the next.
>
> We can choose to walk through it, dragging the carcasses of our prejudice and hatred, our avarice, our data banks and dead ideas, our dead rivers and smoky skies behind us. Or we can walk through lightly, with little luggage, ready to imagine another world. And ready to fight for it. (2020)

In Tremain's *Restoration*, Merivel comically finds his redemption after London has been hit by the plague that turns the world on its head with a Bakhtinian carnivalesque aspect and the ending in the Great Fire. Jeanette Winterson similarly used the historical context of the seventeenth-century plague and the fire of London to parallel her Gargantuan Dog Woman with the rage of her twentieth-century environmental activist who ultimately sets fire to a factory polluting rivers with mercury in *Sexing the Cherry*. In her collection of essays from 1995, *Art Objects*, Winterson notoriously berated realism for its complicity with capitalism and its simple reflection of bland reality. For Winterson, the artist is a visionary who translates the complexity of reality, including its invisible aspects, into imagined worlds. Her writing indeed is more closely related to magic realism as that which upsets the familiar, quotidian, coordinates of the world as we know it. Today what contemporary realism shows however is that the quotidian itself is a site of reinvention and that the complexity of reality can be rendered through combinations of knowledge practices.

Making a narrative out of reality can be scandalous, upsetting. It can take several forms like the novel but also the essay. This was Roy's choice for twenty years and she did not consider it as reportage – the accusation that Winterson levels at realist writing – but as a literary work with form to write about ordinary people and address everyone:

> For each essay, I searched for a form, for language, for structure and narrative. Could I write as compellingly about irrigation as I could about love and loss and childhood? About the salinization of soil? About drainage? Dams? Crops? About structural adjustment and privatization? About the per unit cost of electricity? About things that affect ordinary peoples' lives? Not as reportage, but as a form of storytelling? Was it possible to turn these topics into literature? Literature for everybody – including for people who couldn't read and write, but who had taught me how to think, and could be read to? (2019)

In this speech given in 2019 to PEN America, Roy also reminded her audience of how she has been sued not for the magic realist dimension of her first novel, *The God of Small Things*, but for its realist criticism of the Communist Party's complicity with the Indian caste system. Why bring up Arundhati Roy in this book about British literature? Because the same misapprehension of realism applies in postcolonial studies that have considered the genre to be either a reflection of colonial power or of 'the hegemony of the nation-state' in India for instance (Anjaria 2012: 8). Ulka Anjaria has addressed the issue in

Realism in the Twentieth-Century Indian Novel: Colonial Difference and Literary Form. In her book, she proposes that her 'use of the term "realism" does not merely describe a definable body of texts but also constitutes an epistemic challenge to our accepted literary histories' (2012: 6).

Reconsidering realism, especially realist novels by women writers, means redefining the contemporary literary landscape along new lines of flight. This book has offered to draw parallels between the uses of omniscience and characterization with a view to design new reading communities that dialogue with the world-in-common. Thus realist writing procedures can be reinvested to reconnect with the genre's initial democratic impulse. The mainstream can become minor in the sense of addressing all readers by staging ordinary characters in quotidian relationships. By inviting the readers to engage with individual idiosyncrasies, shared and not shared, sympathetic and antipathetic, the realist novel begs the questions: How do we situate ourselves in the social, scientific, textual communities? How do we collectively inhabit the world? The latter is becoming increasingly urgent and the posthuman traits developed in some of the writers' works studied here outline a change of paradigm in the human perspective on the non-human. Posthuman naturalism reconsiders human nature as kin with non-human species, and nature as nature-cultures. It enlarges the variety of gender relations to relations between kinds raising the question of humane responsibility to multiple others. As Roy said in her speech, literature is a shelter for writers and readers alike which 'softens the borders between men and women, between animals and humans and between life and death' (Roy 2019).

Reinventing realism matters inasmuch as it is a response to the new perceptions of reality that are arising today. It is my contention that it matters more where women writers are concerned in the sense that, considering the prejudices of critical reception, it means taking a firmer stand than their male counterparts. And isn't that the history of feminism in a nutshell: having to assert oneself most vigorously? This book is taking a stand defending the aesthetic choices of women writers by shedding light on the creative process that is singular to each as well as by designing a web of connections that traces new transcorporealities which are given an empirical reality in the novel realist imaginary.

References

Adams, Sarah (2005), 'What a Trip', *The Guardian*, 16 July. Available online: https://www.theguardian.com/books/2005/jul/16/featuresreviews.guardianreview22 (accessed 31 December 2019).

Alaimo, Stacy and Susan, Hekman, eds (2008), *Material Feminisms*, Bloomington and Indianapolis: Indiana University Press.

Alaimo, Stacy (2010), *Bodily Natures: Science, Environment, and the Material Self*, Bloomington and Indianapolis: Indiana University Press.

Alaimo, Stacy (2014), 'Thinking as the Stuff of the World', *O-Zone: A Journal of Object-Oriented Studies*, 1: 13–21.

Alaimo, Stacy (2016), *Exposed: Environmental Politics and Pleasures in Posthuman Times*, Minneapolis and London: University of Minnesota Press.

Anjaria, Ulka (2008), '*On Beauty* and Being Postcolonial: Aesthetics and Form in Zadie Smith', in Tracey L. Walters (ed.), *Zadie Smith: Critical Essays*, 31–56, New York: Peter Lang.

Anjaria, Ulka (2012), *Realism in the Twentieth-Century Indian Novel: Colonial Difference and Literary Form*, Cambridge: Cambridge University Press.

Ardis, Ann (1991), 'Political Attentiveness vs. Political Correctness: Teaching Pat Barker's "Blow Your House Down"', *College Literature*, 18 (3): 44–54.

Armitstead, Claire (2019a), 'Interview Pat Barker: "You could argue that time's up: we're at the end of patriarchy"', *The Guardian*, 4 January. Available online: https://www.theguardian.com/books/2019/jan/04/pat-barker-women-carry-the-can-long-term (accessed 7 March 2019).

Armitstead, Claire (2019b), '"Identity is a pain in the arse": Zadie Smith on Political Correctness', *The Guardian*, 2 February. Available online: https://www.theguardian.com/books/2019/feb/02/zadie-smith-political-correctness-hay-cartagena (accessed 19 March 2019).

(2016), 'A. S. Byatt's New Book Tangles up William Morris with the Opulent Gowns of Fortuny', *Telegraph*, 11 July. Available online: http://www.telegraph.co.uk/books/what-to-read/a-s-byatts-new-book-tangles-up-william-morris-with-the-opulent-g/ (accessed 13 March 2017).

Baker, Timothy C. (2019), *Writing Animals: Language, Suffering, and Animality in Twenty-First Century Fiction*, Cham: Palgrave Macmillan.

Bakhtin, Mikhail (1968), *Rabelais and His World*, trans. Hélène Iswolsky, Cambridge, MA: MIT Press.

Barad, Karen (2003), 'Posthumanist Performativity: Toward an Understanding of How Matter Comes to Matter', *Signs*, 28 (3): 801–31.

Barad, Karen (2007), *Meeting the Universe Halfway: Quantum Physics and the Entanglement of Matter and Meaning*, Durham and London: Duke University Press.

Barad, Karen (2010), 'Quantum Entanglements and Hauntological Relations of Inheritance: Dis/continuities, SpaceTime Enfoldings and Justice to Come', *Derrida Today*, 3 (2): 240–68.

Barker, Pat ([1991/1993/1995] 1998), *The Regeneration Trilogy*, London: Penguin.

Barker, Pat ([1982/1984] 1999), *Union Street & Blow Your House Down*, New York: Picador.

Barker, Pat ([2001] 2002), *Border Crossing*, London: Penguin.

Barker, Pat (2018), *The Silence of the Girls*, London: Hamish Hamilton.

Barthes, Roland (1967), *Writing Degree Zero*, trans. Annette Lavers and Colin Smith, London: Jonathan Cape.

Barthes, Roland (1974), *S/Z*, trans. Richard Miller, Malden and Oxford: Blackwell Publishing.

Barthes, Roland (1989), 'The Reality Effect', in *The Rustle of Language*, trans. Richard Howard, 141–8, Berkeley and Los Angeles: University of California Press.

Bass, Holly (2016), 'Zadie Smith's New Novel Takes on Dance, Fame and Friendship', *The New York Times*, 10 November. Available online: https://www.nytimes.com/2016/11/13/books/review/zadie-smith-swing-time.html 22/03/19 (accessed 22 March 2019).

Baxter, Jeannette and James, David, eds (2014), *Andrea Levy: Contemporary Critical Perspectives*, London and New York: Bloomsbury.

Belsey, Catherine (1992), 'Reading Love Stories', in Joe Andrew (ed.), *Poetics of the Text: Essays to Celebrate Twenty Years of the Neo-Formalist Circle*, 138–52, Amsterdam and Atlanta: Rodopi.

Belsey, Catherine (2002), *Critical Practice*, London and New York: Routledge.

Bennett, Jane (2010), *Vibrant Matter: A Political Ecology of Things*, Durham and London: Duke University Press.

Bentley, Nick (2007), 'Re-writing Englishness: Imagining the Nation in Julian Barnes' *England, England* and Zadie Smith's *White Teeth*', *Textual Practice*, 21 (3): 483–504.

Boccardi, Mariadele (2013), *A. S. Byatt*, Basingstoke and New York: Palgrave Macmillan.

Boyne, John (2016), '*Swing Time* Review: Zadie Smith's New Novel can't Overcome Faults', *The Irish Times*, 12 November. Available online: https://www.irishtimes.com/culture/books/swing-time-review-zadie-smith-s-new-novel-can-t-overcome-faults-1.2858001 (accessed 22 March 2019).

Bradbury, Malcolm and Palmer, David, eds (1979), *The Contemporary English Novel*, London: E. Arnold.

Bradbury, Malcolm (1993), *The Modern British Novel*, London: Secker and Warburg.

Braidotti, Rosi (2002), *Metamorphoses: Towards a Materialist Theory of Becoming*, Cambridge and Malden: Polity.

Braidotti, Rosi (2009), 'Animals, Anomalies, and Inorganic Others', *PMLA*, 124 (2): 526–32.

Braidotti, Rosi (2013), *The Posthuman*, Cambridge and Malden: Polity.

Brannigan, John (2005a), *Pat Barker*, Manchester and New York: Manchester University Press.

Brannigan, John, and Barker, Pat (2005b), 'An Interview with Pat Barker', *Contemporary Literature*, 46 (3): 367–92.

Brooks, Geraldine (2018), 'Giving Voice to Homer's Women', *The New York Times*, 27 September. Available online: https://www.nytimes.com/2018/09/27/books/review/silence-of-the-girls-pat-barker.html (accessed 8 March 2019).

Burri, Julien (2012), 'A. S. Byatt, Grande dame des lettres anglaises', interview at Payot Librairie, February. Available online: https://www

.payot.ch/fr/selections/payot-l%27hebdo-/f-eacute-vrier-2012-les-meilleurs-livres-du-printemps-/entretien-a-s-byatt-grande-dame-des-lettres-anglaises (accessed 3 December 2018).

Buxton, Jackie (1996), '"What's love got to do with it?": Postmodernism and *Possession*', *English Studies in Canada*, 22 (2): 199–219.

Byatt, A. S. ([1990] 1991), *Possession: A Romance*, London: Vintage.

Byatt, A. S. ([1991] 1993), *Passions of the Mind*, London: Vintage International.

Byatt, A. S. ([1993] 1994a), *The Matisse Stories*, London: Vintage.

Byatt, A. S. ([1965] 1994b), *Degrees of Freedom: The Early Novels of Iris Murdoch*, London: Vintage.

Byatt, A. S. ([1985] 1995a), *Still Life*, London: Vintage.

Byatt, A. S. ([1992] 1995b), *Angels and Insects*, London: Vintage.

Byatt, A. S. (1995c), 'In the Grip of Possession', *The Independent*, 2 February. Available online: https://www.independent.co.uk/arts-entertainment/in-the-grip-of-possession-1571141.html (accessed 24 September 2019).

Byatt, A. S. (1998), 'From the Inside, Looking Out', *The Telegraph*, 25 April. Available online: https://www.telegraph.co.uk/culture/4713336/From-the-inside-looking-out.html (accessed 13 September 2019).

Byatt, A. S. ([1998] 1999), *Elementals*, London: Vintage.

Byatt, A. S. (2000a), 'Arachne', in Philip Terry (ed.), *Ovid Metamorphosed*, 131–57, London: Chatto & Windus.

Byatt, A. S. (2000b), 'Strange and Charmed', *New Statesman*, 10 April. Available online: https://www.newstatesman.com/node/151099 (accessed 5 September 2019).

Byatt, A. S. ([2000] 2001a), *The Biographer's Tale*, London: Vintage.

Byatt, A. S. ([2000] 2001b), *On Histories and Stories: Selected Essays*, London: Vintage.

Byatt, A. S. (2003a), 'The Feeling Brain', *Prospect*, 20 June. Available online: http://www.prospectmagazine.co.uk/magazine/thefeelingbrain (accessed 14 March 2017).

Byatt, A. S. (2003b), 'Harry Potter and the Childish Adult', *The New York Times*, 7 July. Available online: https://www.nytimes.com/2003/07/07/opinion/harry-potter-and-the-childish-adult.html (accessed 2 October 2019).

Byatt, A. S. (2004a), *Little Black Book of Stories*, London: Vintage.
Byatt, A. S. ([2003] 2004b), 'Soul Searching', *The Guardian*, 14 February. Available online: https://www.theguardian.com/books/2004/feb/14/fiction.philosophy (accessed 24 October 2016).
Byatt, A. S. (2004c), 'A Child in Time', *The Guardian*, 23 October. Available online: https://www.theguardian.com/books/2004/oct/23/booksforchildrenandteenagers.classics (accessed 2 October 2019).
Byatt, A. S. (2005), 'Dreams and Reality', *Newstatesman*, 11 July. Available online: https://www.newstatesman.com/node/162450 (accessed 2 October 2019).
Byatt, A. S. (2006), 'Observe the Neurones: Between, Above and Below John Donne', *Times Literary Supplement*, 22 September. Available online: http://www.the-tls.co.uk/articles/private/observe-the-neurones/ (accessed 14 March 2017).
Byatt, A. S. (2009), *The Children's Book*, London: Chatto & Windus.
Byatt, A. S. (2010), 'Rose par A.S. Byatt: le spectre du rose', trans. Jean Vaché, *Le Monde des livres*, 22 July. http://www.lemonde.fr/livres/article/2010/07/22/rose-par-a-s-byatt-le-spectre-du-rose_1390851_3260.html (accessed 9 January 2020).
Byatt, A. S. (2011a), *Ragnarok: The End of the Gods*, Edinburgh: Canongate Books.
Byatt, A. S. (2011b), 'The Art of Fiction n°168', interview by Philip Hensher, *The Paris Review* 159.
Byatt, A. S. (2013), 'Sea Story by A. S. Byatt', *The Guardian*, 15 March. Available online: https://www.theguardian.com/books/2013/mar/15/as-byatt-short-story-sea (accessed 5 September 2019).
Byatt, A. S. (2014), 'Porcelain Ghosts: The Secrets of Edmund de Waal's Studio', *The Guardian*, 2 May 2014. Available online: http://www.theguardian.com/artanddesign/2014/may/02/edmund-de-waal-potter-ceramics-essays-as-byatt (accessed 21 May 2014).
Byatt, A. S. (2016), *Peacock and Vine*, London: Chatto & Windus.
Byatt, A. S. (2019), 'A. S. Byatt on Iris Murdoch's *The Bell*', *Literary Hub*, 15 July. Available online: https://lithub.com/a-s-byatt-on-iris-murdochs-the-bell/ (accessed 2 September 2019).
Carter, Angela ([1991] 1992), *Wise Children*, London: Vintage.

Carter, Angela ([1979] 2009), *The Sadeian Woman: An Exercise in Cultural History*, London: Virago.

Chevalier, Jean-Louis (1978), 'Closing Debate', in Presses Universitaires de Caen (ed.), *Rencontres avec Iris Murdoch*, 58–74, Caen: Presses universitaires de Caen.

Chevalier, Jean-Louis (1999), 'Speaking of Sources: An Interview with A. S. Byatt', *Sources*, 6–28.

Cixous, Hélène (1976), 'The Laugh of the Medusa', trans. Keith Cohen and Paula Cohen, *Signs*, 1 (4): 875–93.

Daniel, Lucy (2012), 'Merivel: A Man of His Time by Rose Tremain: Review', *The Independent*, 4 September. Available online: http://www.telegraph.co.uk/culture/books/bookreviews/9509144/Merivel-A-Man-of-His-Time-by-Rose-Tremain-review.html (accessed 17 February 2017).

Dawson, Paul (2009), 'The Return of Omniscience in Contemporary Fiction', *Narrative*, 17 (2): 143–61.

Deleuze, Gilles, and Guattari, Félix (1983), 'What Is a Minor Literature?', trans. Robert Brinkley, *Mississippi Review*, 11 (3): 13–33.

Dodd, Kathryn, and Dodd, Philip (1992), 'From the East End to *EastEnders*: Representations of the Working Class, 1890–1990', in Dominic Strinati and Stephen Wagg (eds), *Come on Down? Popular Media Culture in Post-War Britain*, 116–32. London: Routledge.

Duboin, Corinne (2011), 'Contested Identities: Migrant Stories and Liminal Selves in Andrea Levy's "Small Island"', *Obsidian*, 12 (1): 14–33.

Dwyer, Kate (2019), 'Zadie Smith's New Book Grand Union Is Intensely Personal', *Marie-Claire*, 25 September. Available online: https://www.marieclaire.com/culture/a29214591/zadie-smith-grand-union-interview/ (accessed 3 December 2019).

Eder, Richard (2013), 'Merivel' by Rose Tremain', *The Boston Globe*, 20 January. Available online: https://www.bostonglobe.com/arts/books/2013/04/20/book-review-merivel-man-his-time-rose-tremain/Gth72GD26fHVpkXy9M90IM/story.html (accessed 17 February 2017).

Evaristo, Bernardine (2005), *Soul Tourists*, London: Hamish Hamilton.

Evaristo, Bernardine (2013), *Mr Loverman*, London: Penguin.

Evaristo, Bernardine ([2019] 2020), *Girl, Woman, Other*, London: Penguin.

Eyre, Hermione (2003), 'A. S. Byatt: The Dame Who Dared to Criticize the World of Harry Potter', *The Independent*, 12 July. Available online: https://www.independent.co.uk/news/people/profiles/as-byatt-the-dame-who-dared-to-criticise-the-world-of-harry-potter-95851.html (accessed 2 October 2019).
Felski, Rita (1999), 'The Invention of Everyday Life', *New Formations*, 39: 15–31.
Felski, Rita (2008), *Uses of Literature*, Malden and Oxford: Blackwell.
Felski, Rita (2011), 'Context Stinks!', *New Literary History*, 42 (4): 573–91.
Felski, Rita (2015), *The Limits of Critique*, Chicago: Tthe University of Chicago Press.
Fletcher, Lisa (2016), *Historical Romance Fiction: Heterosexuality and Performativity*, London and New York: Routledge.
Ganteau, Jean-Michel (2003), 'Fantastic but Truthful: The Ethics of Romance', *The Cambridge Quarterley*, 32 (3): 225–38.
Garvey, Anne (2001), 'The Sensual World of Sarah Hall', *The Civilian*, 14 October. Available online: http://civilianglobal.com/arts/sarah-hall-author-lake-district-bbc-national-short-story-award/ (accessed 11 August 2016).
Gąziorek, Andrzej (1995), *Postwar British Fiction: Realism and After*, London: Edward Arnold.
Gifford, Terry (2012), 'Pastoral, Anti-Pastoral and Post-Pastoral as Reading Strategies', in Scott Slovic (ed.), *Critical Insights: Nature and Environment*, 42–61, Ipswich: Salam Press.
Gilbert, Sophie (2018), 'The Silence of Classical Literature's Women', *The Atlantic*, 28 September. Available online: https://www.theatlantic.com/entertainment/archive/2018/09/the-silence-of-the-girls-review-pat-barker/570871/ (accessed 8 March 2019).
Greengrass, Martha (2018), 'The Interview: Pat Barker on The Silence of the Girls', *Waterstones*, blog, 28 September. Available online: https://www.waterstones.com/blog/the-interview-pat-barker-on-the-silence-of-the-girls (accessed 7 March 2019).
Grosz, Elizabeth (1994), *Volatile Bodies: Towards a Corporeal Feminism*, Bloomington: Indiana University Press.
Guignery, Vanessa (2013), 'Zadie Smith's *N/W*: The Novel at an "anxiety crossroads"?', *Études Britanniques Contemporaines*, 45.

Hall, Sarah ([2011] 2012), *The Beautiful Indifference*, London: Faber & Faber.

Hall, Sarah (2015), *The Wolf Border*, London: Faber and Faber.

Hall, Sarah ([2002] 2016), *Haweswater*, London: Faber & Faber.

Hall, Sarah and Hobbes, Peter, eds (2016), *Sex and Death*, London: Faber & Faber.

Hall, Sarah ([2007] 2017a), *The Carhullan Army*, London: Faber and Faber.

Hall, Sarah (2017b), *Madame Zero*, New York: Custom House.

Hall, Sarah (2019), *Sudden Traveller*, London: Faber & Faber.

Hansen, Christiane (2019), 'Indifferent Borders: Confined and Liminal Spaces in Sarah Hall's "Bees"', in Barbara Korte and Laura Ma Lojo-Rodríguez (eds), *Borders and Border Crossings in the Contemporary British Short Story*, 171–86, Cham: Palgrave Macmillan.

Haraway, Donna J. (1988), 'Situated Knowledges: The Science Question in Feminism and the Privilege of Partial Perspective', *Feminist Studies*, 14 (3): 575–99.

Haraway, Donna J. (1991), *Simians, Cyborgs, and Women: The Reinvention of Nature*, New York: Routledge.

Haraway, Donna J. (1997), *Modest_Witness@Second_Millenium. FemaleMan©_Meets_OncoMouse™. Feminism and Technoscience*, New York and London: Routledge.

Haraway, Donna J. (2015), 'Anthropocene, Capitalocene, Plantationocene, Chthulucene: Making Kin', *Environmental Humanities*, 6: 159–65.

Harrison, Christine (2012), 'In Dialogue With the Early Modern Past: Gender Resistance in Rose Tremain's *Restoration* and *Music and Silence*', *European Journal of English Studies*, 16 (03): 227–39.

Harrison, Melissa (2015), *At Hawthorne Time*, London: Bloomsbury.

Harrison, Melissa (2016a), *Rain: Four Walks in English Weather*, London: Faber & Faber.

Harrison, Melissa (2016b), *Spring: An Anthology for the Changing Seasons*, London: Elliott & Thompson.

Harrison, Melissa (2018a), *All Among the Barley*, London: Bloomsbury.

Harrison, Melissa (2018b), 'Escape to the Country: Melissa Harrison on Leaving London Behind for "Deep England"', *The Guardian*, 27 August. Available online: https://www.theguardian.com/books/2018/aug/27/melissa-harrison-escape-to-country-at-hawthorn-time (accessed 17 March 2020).

Harrod, Tanya and Adamson, Glenn (2011), 'Interview with A. S. Byatt', *The Journal of Modern Craft*, 4 (1): 65–82.

Holmes, Christopher (2013), 'The Novel's Third Way: Zadie Smith's Hysterical Realism', in Philip Tew (ed.), *Reading Zadie Smith: The First Decade and Beyond*, 141–53, London and New York: Bloomsbury.

Jakobson, Roman (2003), 'The Metaphoric and Metonymic Poles', in René Dirven and Rafl Pörings (eds), *Metaphor and Metonymy in Comparison and Contrast*, 41–8, Berlin: Walter de Gruyter.

James, David (2008), *Contemporary British Fiction and the Artistry of Space*, London: Continuum.

James, David (2013), 'Wounded Realism', *Contemporary Literature*, 54 (1): 204–14.

James, David (2014), 'The Immediacy of *Small Island*', in Jeanette Baxter and David James (eds), *Andrea Levy: Contemporary Critical Perspectives*, 53–64. London and New York: Bloomsbury.

Jameson, Fredric (2015), *The Antinomies of Realism*, London: Verso.

Kristeva, Julia (1982), *Powers of Horror: An Essay on Abjection*, trans. Leon S. Roudiez, New York: Columbia University Press.

Lang, Anouk (2009), '"Enthralling but at the same time disturbing": Challenging the Readers of *Small Island*', *The Journal of Commonwealth Literature*, 44 (2): 123–40.

Latour, Bruno (1993), *We Have Never Been Modern*, trans. Catherine Porter, Cambridge, MA: Harvard University Press.

Leavitt, David (2010), 'Place of Last Resort', *The New York Times*, 22 October. Available online: https://www.nytimes.com/2010/10/24/books/review/Leavitt-t.html (accessed 19 January 2016).

Ledent, Bénédicte (2016), 'The Many Voices of Poscolonial London: Language and Identity in Zadie Smith's White Teeth (2000) and Andrea Levy's Small Island (2004)', in Janet Wilson and Chris Ringrose (eds), *New Soundings in Postcolonial Writing: Critical and Creative Contours*, 79–93, Leiden and Boston: Brill/Rodopi.

Leith, Sam (2009), 'Writing in Terms of Pleasure: Interview with A. S. Byatt', *The Guardian*, 25 April. Available online: https://www.theguardian.com/books/2009/apr/25/as-byatt-interview (accessed 13 November 2019).

Letissier, Georges (2015), 'Neo-Characterization in the Neo-Victorian Novel', *E-rea*, 13 (1): 1–19.

Levy, Andrea ([2004] 2009), *Small Island*, London: Headline.
Levy, Andrea (2010), *The Long Song*, London: Headline.
Levy, Andrea ([1994] 2016), *Every light in the House Burning*, London: Headline.
Lodge, David (1969), 'The Novelist at the Crossroads', *Critical Quarterly*, 11 (2): 105–32.
Mellor, Mary (2000), 'Feminism and Environmental Ethics: A Materialist Perspective', *Ethics and the Environment*, 5 (1): 107–23.
Menegaldo, Gilles (1998), 'On Art and Life: An Interview with Rose Tremain', *Sources*, 4: 101–19.
Mercer, Kobena, (1987), 'Black Hair/Style Politics', *New Formations*, 3: 33–54.
Moraru, Christian (2011), 'The Forster Connection, or Cosmopolitanism Redux: Zadie Smith's *On Beauty*, *Howards End*, and the Schlegels', *The Comparatist*, 35: 133–47.
Morris, Pam (2003), *Realism*, London and New York: Routledge.
Morton, Timothy (2007), *Ecology Without Nature: Rethinking Environmental Aesthetics*, Cambridge, MA and London: Harvard University Press.
Morton, Timothy (2010), *The Ecological Thought*, Cambridge, MA and London: Harvard University Press.
Moseley, Merrit (2008), *The Fiction of Pat Barker*, London: Palgrave Macmillan.
Moss, Sarah (2009), *Cold Earth*, London: Granta.
Moss, Sarah (2011), *Night Waking*, London: Granta.
Moss, Sarah (2014), *Bodies of Light*, London: Granta.
Moss, Sarah (2015), *Signs for Lost Children*, London: Granta.
Moss, Sarah (2018), *Ghost Wall*, London: Granta.
Moss, Sarah, official website. Available online https://www.sarahmoss.org/about/ (accessed 15 May 2020).
Murdoch, Iris (1961), 'Against Dryness: A Polemical Sketch', *Encounter*, 16: 16–20.
Murray, Douglas (2016), 'Who let A. S. Byatt Publish Peacock and Vine?' *The Spectator*, 9 July. Available online http://www.spectator.co.uk/2016/07/who-let-a-s-byatt-publish-peacock-and-vine/ (accessed 13 March 2017).

Neimanis, Astrida (2009), 'Bodies of Water, Human Rights and the Hydrocommons', *Topia*, 21: 161–82.

Neimanis, Astrida (2013), 'Morning Sickness and Gut Sociality: Towards a Posthumanist Feminist Phenomenology', *Janus Head*, 13 (1): 214–40.

Neimanis, Astrida, and Loewen Walker, Rachel (2014), '*Weathering*: Climate Change and the "Thick Time" of Transcorporeality', *Hypatia* 29 (3): 558–75.

Neimanis, Astrida (2017), *Bodies of Water: Posthuman Feminist Phenomenology*, London and New York: Bloomsbury.

Pelluchon, Corine (2019), *Nourishment: A Philosophy of the Political Body*, trans. Justin E. H. Smith, London and New York: Bloomsbury Academic.

Rancière, Jacques (2010), *Dissensus: On Politics and Aesthetics*, trans. Steven Corcoran, London and New York: Continuum.

Rancière, Jacques ([2004] 2011), *The Politics of Aesthetics: The Distribution of the Sensible*, trans. Gabriel Rockhill, London and New York: Continuum.

Rancière, Jacques (2012), *La leçon d'Althusser*, Paris: La fabrique.

Rancière, Jacques (2014), *Le Fil perdu. Essais sur la fiction moderne*, Paris: La fabrique.

Rawlinson, Mark (2010), *Pat Barker*, Basingstoke and New York: Palgrave Macmillan.

Riley, Charles A. (1995), *Colour Codes: Modern Theories of Color in Philosophy, Painting and Architecture, Literature, Music and Psychology*, Hanover and London: University Press of New England.

Rowell, Charles Henry and Levy, Andrea (2015), 'An Interview with Andrea Levy', *Callaloo*, 38 (2): 258–81.

Roy, Arundhati (2019), 'Literature Provides Shelter: That's Why We Need It', *The Guardian*, 13 May. Available online: https://www.theguardian.com/commentisfree/2019/may/13/arundhati-roy-literature-shelter-pen-america (accessed 14 May 19).

Roy, Arundhati (2020), 'The Pandemic Is a Portal', *The Financial Times*, 3 April. Available online: https://www.ft.com/content/10d8f5e8-74eb-11ea-95fe-fcd274e920ca (accessed 8 April 2020).

Russo, Mary (1995), *The Female Grotesque: Risk, Excess, Modernity*, New York and London: Routledge.

Scarry, Elaine (1998), On Beauty and Being Just, The Tanner Lectures on Human Values, delivered at Yale University, 25–26 March, 78–9. Available online: https://www.google.com/url?sa=t&rct=j&q=&esrc=s&source =web&cd=11&cad=rja&uact=8&ved=2ahUKEwjGxML_tvLiAhUcBGM BHUZkAvQQFjAKegQIABAC&url=https%3A%2F%2Fblogs.aalto.fi %2Fresearchinart%2Ffiles%2F2012%2F10%2FscarryBEAUTY.pdf&usg =AOvVaw0xN6Ujv-RQO2sXUacWxre8 (accessed 18 June 2019).

Sethi, Anita (2019), 'Bernardine Evaristo: "I want to put presence into absence"', *The Guardian*, 27 April. Available online: https://www.theguardian.com/books/2019/apr/27/bernardine-evaristo-girl-woman-other-interview (accessed 17 December 2019).

Smith, Zadie (2000), *White Teeth*, London: Hamish Hamilton.

Smith, Zadie (2001), 'This Is How It Feels to Me', *The Guardian*, 13 October. Available online: https://www.theguardian.com/books/2001/oct/13/fiction.afghanistan (accessed 20 March 2019).

Smith, Zadie (2005), *On Beauty*, London: Hamish Hamilton.

Smith, Zadie (2007), 'Fail Better', *The Guardian*, 13 January.

Smith, Zadie ([2009] 2011), *Changing My Mind*, London: Penguin.

Smith, Zadie (2012), *NW*, London: Hamish Hamilton.

Smith, Zadie (2013), 'Joy', *The New York Review of Books*, 10 January. Available online: https://www.nybooks.com/articles/2013/01/10/joy/ (accessed 6 January 2020).

Smith, Zadie (2017), *Swing Time*, London: Penguin.

Smith, Zadie (2018), 'I Have a Very Messy and Chaotic Mind', *The Guardian*, 21 January. Available online: https://www.theguardian.com/books/2018/jan/21/zadie-smith-you-ask-the-questions-self-doubt (accessed 23 March 2019).

Smith, Zadie (2019a), *Grand Union*, London: Hamish Hamilton.

Smith, Zadie (2019b), 'Fascinated to Presume', *The New York Review of Books*, 24 October. Available online: https://www.nybooks.com/contributors/zadie-smith/ (accessed 27 March 2020).

Sorensen, Sue (2003/4), 'A. S. Byatt and the Life of the Mind: A Response to June Sturrock', *Connotations*, 13 (1–2): 180–90.

Sorensen, Sue (2015), 'Rose Tremain', *The Literary Encyclopedia*. Available online: http://www.litencyc.com/php/speople.php?rec=true&UID=4447 (accessed 12 November 2016).

Steffens, Karolyn (2014), 'Communicating Trauma: Pat Barker's Regeneration Trilogy and W. H. R. Rivers's Psychoanalytic Method', *Journal of Modern Literature*, 37 (3): 36–55.

Sturrock, June (2010), 'Artists as Parents in A. S. Byatt's *The Children's Book* and Iris Murdoch's *The Good Apprentice*', *Connotations*, 20 (1): 108–30.

Tallis, Raymond (1988), *In Defence of Realism*, Lincoln and London: University of Nebraska Press.

Terry, Philip, ed. (2000), *Ovid Metamorphosed*, London: Chatto & Windus.

Tonkin, Boyd (1994), 'Interview with A.S. Byatt', *Anglistik: International Journal of English Studies*, 10: 15–26.

Tortorici, Dayna (2016), 'Zadie Smith's Dance of Ambivalence', *The Atlantic*, December. Available online: https://www.theatlantic.com/magazine/archive/2016/12/zadie-smiths-dance-of-ambivalence/505832/ (accessed 22 March 2019).

Tremain, Rose ([1978] 1999a), *Letter to Sister Benedicta*, London: Vintage.

Tremain, Rose ([1983] 1999b), *The Colonel's Daughter and Other Stories*, London: Vintage.

Tremain, Rose ([1999] 2000), *Music and Silence*, London: Vintage.

Tremain, Rose ([2003] 2004), *The Colour*, London: Vintage.

Tremain, Rose ([1989] 2009), *Restoration*, London: Vintage.

Tremain, Rose (2010), 'Rose Tremain, the Orange Prize Winning Author on Her New Novel "Trespass"', *The Scotsman*, 26 February. Avalable online: https://www.scotsman.com/arts-and-culture/books/interview-rose-tremain-the-orange-prize-winning-author-on-her-new-novel-trespass-1-792563 (accessed 11 July 2016).

Tremain, Rose (2013), 'Rose Tremain Discusses the Inspirations for Merivel', *The Telegraph*, 1 June. Available online: https://www.telegraph.co.uk/culture/books/authorinterviews/10076021/Rose-Tremain-discusses-the-inspirations-for-Merivel.html (accessed 13 May 2015).

Tuana, Nancy (2008), 'Viscous Porosity: Witnessing Katrina', in Stacy Alaimo and Susan J. Hekman (eds), *Material Feminisms*, 188–213, Bloomington: Indiana University Press.

Turner, Nick (2010), *Post-War British Women Novelists and the Canon*, London and New York: Continuum.

Turner, Nick (2013), 'Realism, Women Writers and the Contemporary British Novel', in Dorothee Birke and Stella Butter (eds), *Realisms in Contemporary Culture: Theories, Politics and Medial Configurations*, 49–69, Boston and Berlin: Walter de Gruyter.

Upstone, Sara (2017), *Rethinking Race and Identity in Contemporary British Fiction*, London and New York: Routledge.

Urano, Kaoru (2012), 'From the Country House to the Painting: An "Aesthetic" Adaptation of *Howards End* in Zadie Smith's *On Beauty*', *Textes et contextes*, 7. Available online: https://preo.u-bourgogne.fr/textesetcontextes/index.php?id=359 (accessed 5 December 2019).

Vice, Sue (1997), *Introducing Bakhtin*, Manchester and New York: Manchester University Press.

Ward, Elizabeth (1983), 'On the Seamy Side of the Street', *The Washington Post*, 18 September. Available online: https://www.washingtonpost.com/archive/entertainment/books/1983/09/18/on-the-seamy-side-of-the-street/b1a55bb7-75d9-4ede-83ec-815a434db667/ (accessed 17 October 2019).

Wells, Lynn (2003), *Allegories of Telling: Self-Referential Narratives in Contemporary British Fiction*, Amsterdam and New York: Rodopi.

Wilson, Emily (2018), 'The Silence of the Girls by Pat Barker Review – A Feminist Iliad', *The Guardian*, 22 August. Available online: https://www.theguardian.com/books/2018/aug/22/silence-of-the-girls-pat-barker-book-review-iliad (accessed 8 March 2019).

Wood, James (2000), 'Human, All Too Inhuman', *The New Republic*, 24 July. Available online: https://newrepublic.com/article/61361/human-inhuman. (accessed 25 January 2019).

Wood, James (2009a), 'James Wood Writes about the Manipulations of Ian McEwan', *London Review of Books*, 31 (8), 30 April. Available online: https://www.lrb.co.uk/v31/n08/james-wood/james-wood-writes-about-the-manipulations-of-ian-mcewan (accessed 25 September 2019).

Wood, James (2009b), 'Bristling with Diligence', *London Review of Books*, 31 (9), 8 October. Available online: https://www.lrb.co.uk/v31/n19/james-wood/bristling-with-diligence (accessed 25 September 2019).

Woodward, Kathleen, ed. (1999), *Figuring Age: Women, Bodies, Generations*, Bloomington: Indiana University Press.

Woolf, Virginia (1942), 'Middlebrow', in Hogarth Press (ed.), *The Death of the Moth*, 113–19, London: Hogarth Press.

Younge, Gary and Levy, Andrea (2010), 'Interview. "I started to realise what fiction could be: And I thought, wow! You can take on the world"', *The Guardian*, 30 January. Available online: https://www.theguardian.com/books/2010/jan/30/andrea-levy-long-song-interview (accessed 3 April 2020).

Zola, Émile (1893), *The Experimental Novel and Other Essays*, trans. Belle M. Sherman, New York: Cassell Publishing.

Index

agential realism 8, 130
Alaimo, Stacy 5, 8–9, 91–2, 131, 147
Althusser, Louis 5, 12, 53
analogy 16, 18, 108, 113, 119, 132–4
Anjaria, Ulka 72, 154–5
anthropomorphism, anthropomorphic, anthropomorphizing 18, 119, 124, 132, 134
Ardis, Ann 50–1
Austen, Jane 32

Baker, Timothy 121–2
Bakhtin, Mikhail 13, 43–4
Balzac, Honoré de 14, 44, 47, 51
Barad, Karen 5, 7–9, 83–4, 92, 106, 108, 112, 130–1
Barker, Pat
  Another World 96
  Blow Your House Down 15, 48–50, 57, 150
  Border Crossing 48
  Life Class trilogy 51
  Regeneration trilogy 51, 64
  The Silence of the Girls 56–9
  Union Street 48–9, 59–60, 63, 93–6, 99–100
Barthes, Roland 5, 11–12, 17, 21, 23, 63, 67, 75, 91, 94
becoming(s) 116, 120, 122–3, 130, 132–3, 145–6
Belsey, Catherine 3, 11–12, 14
Bennett, Jane 8, 10, 119, 123–5, 127
Bentley, Nick 70–1
Boccardi, Mariadele 38

Bradbury, Malcolm 21–2
Braidotti, Rosi 6, 18, 92, 116, 118–19, 124, 132, 134, 146
Brannigan, John 14, 63, 95, 150
Breton, André 48
Brexit 18, 138, 141, 143
Buxton, Jackie 3
Byatt, A. S.
  'Arachne' 29, 77
  'Art Work' 108–9
  The Biographer's Tale 75–7
  The Children's Book 28, 30, 38–40
  Christ in the House of Mary and Martha' 108–9
  Degrees of Freedom 34–6
  'embodied mind' 6, 29, 75
  'Medusa's Ankles' 102–4
  'Morpho Eugenia' 132–3
  On Histories and Stories 90, 132
  Peacock and Vine 28–9, 35, 78–9
  'People in Paper Houses' 21–2, 27
  'The Pink Ribbon' 87–8
  Possession 3, 21, 27, 108, 139
  'Raw Material' 109–11
  'Sea Story' 8, 18, 126–8, 134, 148
  'self-conscious realism' 89
  Still Life 88–9
  'A Stone Woman' 8, 18, 122–5
  Ragnarok 18, 28–9, 35, 76–8, 127–9, 131, 148
  A Whistling Woman 75, 89

Carter, Angela 14, 44, 49, 87, 103, 134
Chabrol, Claude 47

Chevalier, Jean-Louis 28–9, 37, 40, 76
Cixous, Hélène 44

Dawson, Paul 27, 70–1
Deleuze, Gilles 116–18, 120, 146
democracy, democratic 1, 10–11, 17, 42, 44, 49, 66, 92, 112, 116–17, 155
Dickens, Charles 14, 30, 46–7, 51, 147
distribution of the sensible 13, 26, 32, 91, 116
Douglas, Mary 95
Duboin, Corinne 56, 66

Eliot, George 6, 12, 23–6, 30, 33
entanglement(s) 8, 92, 99, 106, 110, 115, 133
Evaristo, Bernardine
  The Emperor's Babe 138
  Girl, Woman, Other 96–7, 100, 104, 117
  Mr Loverman 101, 105–6
  Soul Tourist 96, 99, 138

Felski, Rita 13, 15, 19, 26, 53–4, 64, 66, 147, 150–2
Fletcher, Lisa 3
Forster, E. M. 71–2
Fowles, John 21, 28
Freud, Sigmund 33, 64

Ganteau, Jean-Michel 115
Garnett, David 120–1
Gasiorek, Andrzej 3
Gifford, Terry 139
Grosz, Elizabeth 17, 93, 95
Guignery, Vanessa 36

Hall, Sarah
  'Bees' 8, 118–20, 134, 141
  The Carhullan Army 82–5, 118
  The Electric Michelangelo 134
  'Evie' 87
  Haweswater 81–4, 113–16, 118–19, 134
  'M' 131
  'Mrs Fox' 8, 120–2
  'Sudden Traveller' 141
  The Wolf Border 80, 82, 85, 118, 134, 140
Hansen, Christiane 118
Haraway, Donna 6–7, 9–10, 16, 67–8, 71, 73–5, 77–8, 82, 89, 112, 122, 131, 133, 148
Hardy, Thomas 50
Harrison, Christine 62
Harrison, Melissa
  All Among the Barley 138, 140
  At Hawthorne Time 140
  Rain. Four Walks in English Weather 19, 144–6
  Spring. An Anthology for the Changing Seasons 146–7, 153
Holmes, Christopher 23, 25–6
hysterical realism 12, 31

Irigaray, Luce 9, 17, 93
Ishiguro, Kazuo 46

James, David 36, 50–1, 65, 152
James, Henry 23
Jameson, Fredrick 26
Joyce, James 36

Kristeva, Julia (abject, abjection) 13, 17, 43–4, 53, 93, 95

Lacan, Jacques 5, 43, 53–4
Lang, Anouk 15, 64–5
Latour, Bruno 8, 10, 26
Lefebvre, Henri 115
Lent, Bénédicte 117–18
Letissier, Georges (neo-characterization) 14, 46
Levy, Andrea
  Every Light in the House Burning 104–5
  The Long Song 151–2

Small Island 15, 54–6, 60, 64–6, 106–7, 118
Lodge, David 22–3

McEwan, Ian 31
magic realism 14, 44, 154
material-semiotic nodes 6–7, 16–17, 49, 63, 104, 112
Mellor, Mary 80, 82
Menegaldo, Gilles 68
Mercer, Kobena 104–7
metonymy 10, 102, 108, 122, 124
Me Too 19, 140, 149
Moraru, Christian 72
Morris, Pam 4
Morton, Timothy 9, 10
Moseley, Merritt 59, 64
Moss, Sarah
  Bodies of Light 139
  Cold Earth 137
  Ghost Wall 137–8, 140
  Night Waking 139–40
  Signs for Lost Children 139
Murdoch, Iris 12, 22, 30, 32–5, 37–40, 88

Nabokov, Vladimir 23, 33, 36
naturalism, naturalist 13–14, 18, 45, 47–8, 51, 59, 115, 130–1, 155
Neimanis, Astrida 17, 19, 83, 113, 131, 145–6

onto-stories 8, 125, 148

Pelluchon, Corinne 129–31, 134
phenomenology 15, 17–19, 50, 66, 113, 129, 131, 134, 144, 146
post-pastoral 138, 145

Rancière, Jacques 10, 12–13, 17, 23–6, 32, 44, 49, 56, 91–2, 147
Rawlinson, Mark 45, 49
readerly/writerly 11–12, 14, 23, 34–6, 108

Riley, Charles 101
Rowling, J. K. 38–40
Roy, Arundhati 117, 153–5
Russo, Mary 13, 44

Scarry, Elaine 35, 74
Smith, Zadie
  The Autograph Man 37
  'Blocked' 69
  Changing My Mind 23–5, 70, 150
  Feel Free 38
  'The Lazy River' 141–4, 150
  'Now More Than Ever' 149
  NW 36–7, 70, 73
  On Beauty 35, 70, 72–3
  Swing Time 36–7, 70, 73–4, 80–1, 85–7, 97–9, 104–5
  White Teeth 12, 70–1, 117
Sorensen, Sue 4, 53, 75, 78, 89
Spinoza, Baruch (Spinozist, monism) 6, 8, 23, 25, 29, 123
Steffens, Karolyn 64
Sturrock, June 40

Taine, Hippolyte 45
Tallis, Raymond 3, 12–13
taxonomy, taxonomic 6, 8, 17, 107–8, 122, 124, 128, 131, 133, 139, 148
transcorporeality, transcorporeal 9, 84, 91–2, 156
Tremain, Rose
  The Colour 50–1, 111–12
  Letter to Sister Benedicta 52, 117
  Merivel: A Man of His Time 52–3
  Music and Silence 60–2
  "My Love Affair with James I" 68
  Restoration 51–3, 62, 153
  The Road Home 52, 62, 117
  Sacred Country 62, 153
  Sadler's Birthday 46–7

The Swimming Pool
    Season 47, 62, 118
    Trespass 47–8
Tuana, Nancy (viscous porosity) 9, 17, 94, 110–11
Turner, Nick 4, 5

Upstone, Sara 96
Urano, Kaoru 73

weathering 19, 83, 145–6
Wells, Lynn 21
Winterson, Jeanette 153–4
Wood, James 12, 25, 30–2, 38
Woodward, Kathleen 102
Woolf, Virginia 15, 30, 33

Zola, Émile 14, 45, 47–9, 51, 130–1

www.ingramcontent.com/pod-product-compliance
Lightning Source LLC
Chambersburg PA
CBHW061837300426
44115CB00013B/2421